Good Food for Camp and Trail

Good Food
for Camp & Trail

All-Natural Recipes
for Delicious
Meals Outdoors

Dorcas S. Miller

PRUETT PUBLISHING COMPANY
BOULDER, COLORADO

Printed in the United States
03 02 01 00 5

Library of Congress Cataloging-in-Publication Data

Miller, Dorcas S., 1949–
    Good food for camp and trail : a guide to planning and
preparing delicious all-natural meals outdoors / Dorcas S. Miller.
        p. cm.
    Includes bibliographical references and index.
    ISBN 0-87108-811-8 (pb)
    1. Outdoor cookery. 2. Camping—Equipment and supplies.
3. Nutrition. I. Title.
TX823.M535   1993
641.5'78—dc20   92-38281
                                                                      CIP

Book and cover design by Jody Chapel, Cover to Cover Design
Cover illustration by Kathleen Nichols-Lanzoni
Illustrations by Milford Cushman and Dawn Peterson

To my mother,
who taught me how to cook.

Contents

Acknowledgments

I owe a hearty thank-you to Kathy, Faloon, Bergie, Ruthie, Karen, Sue, Marnie, Betsy, Sheila, Thea, and my husband, Ben, for testing recipes and products. Ben gets a gold star for eating from my test kitchen without complaint.

I also owe a special thank-you to the reference librarians at the Maine State Library, who helped me locate books and articles from all over the country.

Introduction

In 1972, when I worked for Outward Bound in Texas, we had three different trail dinners: neon macaroni and cheese, turkey tetrazzini, and a third alternative that I have mercifully forgotten. The macaroni was the least bad of the three, so I traded my other dinners and subsisted on macaroni and powdered cheese for the summer. I'm surprised I didn't glow in the dark.

Those months of prepackaged trail food made me resolve that I would never eat it again. In subsequent jobs as a trip leader, and on personal trips, I stuck with "real" food, heavy though it was. I also put together nutritional information, menu suggestions, and recipes emphasizing whole foods in *The Healthy Trail Food Book*, first published in 1976.

Now, many years later, I find that a lot has changed. Dinners like shrimp alfredo, mountain chili, and honey-lime chicken line the shelves in backpacking stores, and an impressive variety of all-natural items is available through mail order.

The general marketplace has changed as well. Many companies now offer products that are easy to prepare and free of unhealthy preservatives. Supermarket and health-food store shelves are stocked with dry mixes for refries, hummus, curry rice, instant soup, vegetarian chili, and wheat pilaf. In other aisles, there are boxes of whole-wheat biscuit mix, muesli, and granola.

Good Food for Camp and Trail reflects these changes. It offers many recipes but also includes detailed information about the price, weight, and nutrients of specialty backpacking foods and lightweight foods found in super-markets and health-food stores.

This book emphasizes foods that are widely available. I live in rural Maine, so I do not have access to the large natural-food stores and ethnic grocery stores that are found in most urban areas. My assumption is that if I can find products or order them through the mail, then you can, too. In fact, you may have access to a much wider selection than I have.

This book is designed to be used in many different ways. If you are looking for information on prepackaged foods, skip the recipes and go straight to the chapters on backpacking and supermarket foods. If you love to cook, spend more time with the recipes and the section about cooking on trail. If you are planning a strenuous trip, be sure to check out the nutrition section and the charts giving nutritional information. If you are new to outdoor cuisine, browse through the entire book and return to the sections of interest.

I have used "all natural" in the spirit rather than the narrow definition of the term. Strictly speaking, all natural ingredients would be ones that are derived entirely from natural sources. But some natural ingredients may not be good for us, while some synthetic ingredients do us no harm. This book focuses on recipes and products that do not contain ingredients that should be used with caution or avoided altogether. (See Chapter 2 for further explanation and a list of red-flag additives.)

In a few instances I have received and reviewed products that contain these additives. I have included these products in the book as a way of saying, "Let the buyer beware." Different companies use different standards to define "all natural." You—the consumer—can make your own decision about where you draw the line and what you want to eat. This book simply gives you information to use in making that decision.

As I was writing this book, I ran across a 1979 review of *The Healthy Trail Food Book* from a national outdoor magazine. "The emphasis is on natural foods, but with a bit more cereal and starch than is good for well-balanced and nutritious meals," the reviewer wrote. I had to chuckle. Nutritionists now recommend that we obtain 58 percent of our calories from carbohydrates—the very cereals and starches that the reviewer rejected. The food pyramid, with carbohydrates forming the base, has clearly replaced the "basic four" food groups, which encouraged high-fat, high-protein diets.

I did a quick calculation of the number of days I have spent on trail and, combined, they total over two and a half years. What a lot of food! Some was bad, most was good. I learned a great deal along the way, and I hope that you can profit from my experience. I discovered, as a Maine Guide, that the two most important aspects of a trip are the food and the weather. You can't do much about the weather, but you certainly can do a lot about the food.

Dorcas Susan Miller
Chelsea, Maine

1
Planning Food for the Trail

Nutrition, caloric needs, weight, cooking time, ease of preparation, and cost are all important considerations when planning food for a camping trip. So before you start making a shopping list, jot down answers to some key questions.

Who is going on the trip and what are their needs? On the average, men require one-third more calories than do women. Teenagers need 10 percent more calories than do adults—and will always be hungry for more. If people don't like a food, there is no sense in putting it on the menu. Individuals with food allergies or special food preferences need to be accommodated.

What kind of trip is planned? If you are setting up a base camp and taking day hikes, you'll need fewer calories than if you are hiking the Appalachian Trail. If you are doing a float trip on a river, you'll be using less energy than if you are running rapids and portaging a canoe.

What are the constraints on weight? If you are planning a biking, sea-kayaking, or backpacking trip, where space and weight are at a premium, then you'll want to choose lightweight foods. If you are setting out on that float trip, you can pack fresh fruit, vegetables, and cheese in a cooler, letting the canoe or raft carry the weight.

Will you be cooking on a gas stove? If you have to carry fuel and you are going any distance, then you'll want to plan meals that are economical of fuel.

Does your itinerary include short relaxed days or long strenuous ones? If you anticipate making camp early, you can plan meals that require more preparation. If you are going to be going hard all day, though, you may want to choose meals that are quick and easy to prepare.

What is your budget? The more work someone else has put into preparing the food, the more it is going to cost.

Nutritional Needs

The following recommended daily dietary allowances for calories and protein are designed for ordinary activity. For many adults, that means sedentary activity.

Requirements for Calories and Protein *(Sedentary Activity)*

	Age	Weight (pounds)	Height (inches)	Calories	Grams Protein
Males	11–14	99	62	2,700	45
	15–18	145	69	2,800	56
	19–22	154	70	2,900	56
	23–50	154	70	2,700	56
	51–75	154	70	2,400	56
	76 +	154	70	2,050	56
Females	11–14	101	62	2,200	46
	15–18	120	64	2,100	46
	19–22	120	64	2,100	44
	23–50	120	64	2,000	44
	51–75	120	64	1,800	44
	76 +	120	64	1,600	44

Figures set by Food and Nutrition Board, National Academy of Sciences–National Research Council.

A hiker, though, who covers three miles on roads and ten miles cross-country with a gain of 2,500 feet in elevation, might burn 4,100 calories (Ferber 1974). A person on a winter trip who spends four hours walking on packed snow with an 11-pound pack and another four hours skiing on a packed trail with a heavy pack might use over 4,300 calories per day.[1] A member of a Himalayan expedition might need 5,000 to 6,000 calories per day.[2] The U.S. Army sets 4,500 calories per day as its cold-weather target.[3] The National Outdoor Leadership School calculates 2,500 to 3,000 calories per day for normal outdoor activity, 3,000 to 3,700 calories per day for winter camping, and 3,700 to 4,500 calories per day for extremely demanding mountaineering (Sukey, Orr, and Lindholm 1991).

Approximate Number of Calories Used per Hour

Weight (in pounds)	100	120	150	180	200
Backpacking (40-pound pack)	307	348	410	472	513
Canoeing (4 mph)	276	344	414	504	558
Hiking	225	255	300	345	375
Mountain Climbing	450	510	600	690	750
Skiing, Cross-Country	525	595	700	805	875
Walking	204	258	318	372	426

From *Fitness for Life*, 2nd ed. Charles B. Corbin and Ruth Lindsey (Glenview, Ill.: Scott, Foresman and Company, 1985).

Nutrients

We get energy from proteins, carbohydrates, and fats, and fats are by far the greatest source of energy per unit of weight. Both proteins and carbohydrates contain 4 calories per gram and fat contains 9 calories per gram.

Proteins

Proteins are made of building blocks called amino acids. These amino acids are used to rebuild body tissue. They

---

1. E. W. Askew, "Nutrition for a Cold Environment," *The Physician and Sportsmedicine* 17, no. 12 (December 1989).

2. N. Clark, "Expedition Nutrition: Tips for Menu Planning," *Climbing* (August 1986).

3. U.S. Department of the Army, "Nutritional Allowances Standards and Education," Army Regulation 40–25 (Washington, D.C.: Department of the Army, 1985).

also provide energy, serve as catalysts for metabolic reactions, and make hormones. In general, the need for protein is constant, although psychological stress or physical stress, such as hard work that increases muscle mass, can increase the demand (Lappé 1991). The body cannot use a full day's complement of protein at one time, so protein intake must be spread over the course of a day.

Carbohydrates

Carbohydrates supply calories in a quickly usable form and are necessary to various metabolic functions. They provide quick energy rather than staying power. There are two types of carbohydrates: simple, such as the sugars in fruits and vegetables; and complex, such as the starches in grains, pasta, bread, and beans. Carbohydrates have received greater dietary emphasis as the recommended percentages of protein and fats have decreased over the years.

Fats

Fats supply fat-soluble vitamins and a high concentration of calories. Because they are not quickly digested, fats provide a sense of fullness. Along with proteins, they release energy over a long period of time and are particularly important in long-term strenuous activity and in cold weather.

Vitamins and Minerals

Various vitamins and minerals are essential to the body's proper functioning. Adequate amounts can be obtained through a balanced diet. However, on long trips, with little or no fresh food, combination vitamin-and-mineral tablets may be the easiest way to ensure getting enough of these essential nutrients.

Water

Water is not a nutrient, but without it we would die. In summer, drink a minimum of two to three quarts per day. In winter or at altitude, drink three to five or even more quarts per day. If you are not taking regular pit stops; if your urine is not "gin clear" (except during the several hours after you have taken a vitamin-and-mineral tablet);

or if you feel tired, have a headache, feel nauseous, or have muscle cramps, drink liquids and increase your overall intake of liquids. If you find that you are urinating frequently and that drinking liquids does not slake your thirst, check your salt intake.

Sources of Calories

The recommended source percentages for calories for the general public, as set by the U.S. Senate Select Committee on Human Needs, are 12 percent from proteins, 58 percent from carbohydrates, and 30 percent from fats. Most of the carbohydrate calories should come from complex carbohydrates, with some from naturally occurring sugars. If you eat a diet that emphasizes complex carbohydrates, you probably have an appropriate balance.

These figures may be adjusted somewhat for outdoor activities. According to one authority, a balance of 15 percent of a day's calories from proteins, 52 percent from carbohydrates, and 33 percent from fats is appropriate for general outdoor trips.[4] For cold-weather conditions, an even higher percentage of fat is allowable, as long as a minimum for carbohydrates and proteins is met.[5] (Research also shows that when you camp in winter, you can keep your toes warmer at night by eating a snack of 600 to 1,200 calories just before going to sleep.)

At altitude, fats are often unappealing and both fats and proteins are hard to digest, so a large percentage of calories must come from carbohydrates. The recommended balance for Himalayan-type expeditions, for example, is 10 to 20 percent of calories from protein, 60 to 70 percent from carbohydrates, and the balance from fats (Gunn 1988).

Sample Day

How do we apply this nutritional information to planning the food for a camping trip? Let's look at a sample day.

---

4. C. R. Consolazio and D. D. Schnakenberg, "Nutrition and the Response to Extreme Environments." Federal Proceedings, vol. 36, no. 5, 1977.
5. "Nutrition for a Cold Environment."

We'll assume that Bob, who weighs 154 pounds, will need 4,200 calories per day, including at least 56 grams of protein. Sue, who weighs 120 pounds, will need 3,500 calories, including at least 44 grams of protein.

Sample Day, Amounts per Person

	Calories	Protein (grams)	Carbohydrate (grams)	Fat (grams)
Breakfast				
instant oatmeal, 2 pkts	276	10	46	6
sugar, 1 T	40	0	11	0
instant nonfat milk, 1/3 c	164	16	24	trace
1 c coffee	4	trace	1	0
Snacks				
dried apples, 10 rings	155	1	42	trace
granola bars, 2	240	4	34	10
hard candy, 1 oz	110	0	28	trace
Lunch				
pilot crackers, 4	240	4	40	8
peanut butter, 2 T	190	8	6	16
almonds, scant 1/4 c	167	6	6	15
milk chocolate, 1 oz	145	2	16	9
Dinner				
chicken soup, mix	220	8	33	6
macaroni and cheese,				
mix, 1-1/2 c	600	16	68	30
peas and onions, freeze				
dried, 3/4 c	111	6	21	1
fig bars, 4	200	4	44	4
herb tea	5	trace	trace	trace
with honey, 2 t	44	trace	18	0
TOTAL	**2,913**	**85**	**438**	**105**
		11%	*58%*	*31%*
A: Additional food (both Bob and Sue)				
bagel	165	6	30	2
jam, 2 T	110	trace	28	trace
raisins, 1/4 c	120	1	32	trace
cheese, 1 oz	115	7	1	9
milk chocolate, 1 oz	145	2	16	9
NEW TOTAL FOR SUE	**3,568**	**101**	**545**	**125**
		11%	*59%*	*30%*

Sample Day, Amounts per Person *(continued)*

	Calories	Protein (grams)	Carbohydrate (grams)	Fat (grams)
B: Extra food for Bob				
pilot crackers, 4	240	4	40	8
peanut butter, 3 T	285	12	9	24
almonds, scant 1/4 c	167	6	6	15
NEW TOTAL FOR BOB	**4,260**	**123**	**600**	**172**
		11%	*54%*	*35%*

Analysis of Day

Both Bob and Sue get enough protein with the original menu, and the caloric sources (11% from protein, 58% from carbohydrate, and 31% from fat) are quite close to the recommended amounts. The calorie count, though, is not high enough for either person.

If Sue and Bob add more food (A on chart) and Bob gets an extra ration (B on chart), they'll both get enough calories, roughly from the recommended sources. If they found that their protein grams just barely met the requirement, either because of food preferences or allergies, they could increase protein by eating foods in certain combinations. (See Chapter 10 for an explanation of protein complementarity.)

The point of this sample day is to show that, for most outdoor trips, calories are the key. If you plan a varied menu that gives you the number of calories you need per day, you are likely to get enough protein and achieve a reasonable balance among proteins, carbohydrates, and fats—so do not spend too much time with the calculator. The charts in Chapter 6 provide information about the nutritional content of many foods, and you can learn a lot by browsing through them, but it is not necessary to be a fanatic about every last calorie.

However, if you're planning a winter trip, a trip to the mountains, or an expedition where physical demands will be high and resupplies infrequent, you may want to calculate more closely to make sure that you and your companions won't be stranded. Even then, calculating several representative days will probably be sufficient to ensure that you're on track.

The National Outdoor Leadership School (NOLS) uses a much different and much simpler method for planning food. NOLS sends students out with a combination of heavier supermarket foods and lighter dehydrated items. The school calculates calories by weight of food, using these guidelines: 1-1/2 to 2 pounds per person per day yields 2,500 to 3,000 calories; 2 to 2-1/4 pounds per day yields 3,000 to 3,700 calories; and 2-1/4 to 2-1/2 pounds per day yields 3,700 to 4,500 calories (Richard, Orr, and Lindholm 1988). My own experience packing out trips supports these figures.

Weight: How to Lighten the Load

If weight is an issue on your trip and you are cooking on a gas stove, then you'll need to choose food that is both lightweight and quick-cooking. In general, freeze-dried entrees require no cooking, just the addition of boiling water. Dried foods can be rehydrated slowly in water at air temperature (ten minutes to an hour or more, depending on the food), or more quickly in hot or boiling water. If you are willing to carry the food while it rehydrates, you can have a hot meal using very little gas.

Many supermarket foods cook quickly. Instant oatmeal and instant soups require only the addition of boiling water. Grain products like pasta, couscous, and bulgur take much less time to cook than do whole grains. Decorticated lentils cook more quickly than do whole lentils. In fact, all-natural quick-cooking entrees—products developed for the fast-paced American lifestyle—usually contain precooked brown rice, couscous, or bulgur. Cooking time can also be shortened for some foods by presoaking, or by removing the pot from heat a few minutes early and letting the food finish cooking on its own.

There are other ways to decrease cooking time. If you have a food mill, you can mill rice and lentils to break or grind them into smaller pieces that will cook more quickly. I milled about a quarter of the grain-based dinners on a seven-week canoe trip in Canada as a hedge against running short of fuel. I have also used a lightweight pressure cooker, which can shorten cooking time for grains and legumes by one-third to one-half.

When cooking on a stove, use as much heat as you need but no more; the stove uses less fuel when it's on low than when it's on high. It is critical, of course, to use a stove with a "low" setting.

Place the stove so that it is screened from the wind. You can put your kitchen in the lee of some rocks, a canoe, or a couple of packs. Some stoves come with a windscreen, but be careful not to use a windscreen on a stove that is not designed for it. If too much heat builds up, such a stove can explode.

On trail, there tend to be times when the stove is running but there is nothing on it—when someone is going for water, for example, or between courses. Have a pot of water ready to go on the stove as soon as it is lit, and keep a lid on the pot to conserve heat. Since it is inconvenient to stop the stove and start it again, plan ahead so that you will always have the next pot ready to put on as soon as the previous pot is off. If you're not quite organized, put on the hot-drinks water for any intervening time so the stove's heat will not be wasted. Saving two or three minutes worth of fuel at each meal adds up by the end of a week-long trip.

The efficiency of stoves varies, so the best way to calculate how much gas you will need is to figure out how long a tank of gas for your stove lasts. You may need to factor in whether you usually run the stove on the high or the low setting. The National Outdoor Leadership School uses a general formula of one-sixth quart per person per day, and two and a half times that amount in the winter (Richard, Orr, and Lindholm 1988).

When you have completed your menu, estimate how much gas you will need each day, then add extra fuel for cleanup and for a safety margin.

Planning a Menu:
What Do You Like to Eat?

Your best clue to planning trail food is to consider what you and your traveling companions eat at home. Do you prefer gourmet meals to simple one-pot entrees? Do you eat the same breakfast several days in a row? Do you enjoy cooking? Are any foods sacrosanct, such as a special brand of coffee or tea? Does anyone in the group have food allergies or dietary restrictions? Can the foods you eat at home be adapted to the trail?

When you are planning your menu, be realistic. If you enjoy cooking and regularly whip up elaborate meals at home, then go ahead and plan a couple of high-cuisine meals on the trail. But if you don't particularly enjoy cooking, then being out in nature will probably not change your inclination.

Even if you are anticipating a slow trip with lots of time for cooking, plan a couple of meals that are easy and quick. Inevitably something comes up—it's raining or you get windbound and need to make up the time or you need a quick breakfast so you can get an early start.

Plan foods and meals that you've had before and that everyone on the trip will enjoy. Don't take something because "it's good for you" or because you think it'll taste better on trail. Build character some other way.

Food is even more important on trail than it is at home. Food gives you the calories to hike, bike, kayak, or do whatever activity you've planned, but it also feeds morale. A hot mug of Earl Grey tea on a cold morning, a handful of gorp and jerky when lunch stretches into the distance, or a big bowl of pasta at the end of a hard day all make a difference to your psyche as well as to your body.

Besides, food is a key part of how we relate to one another. Meals provide us with a chance to talk about what has happened and what lies ahead. If there is not enough food, or if the food is unappealing, spirits can sink.

As I wrote in the Introduction, weather and food are perceived as two of the most important elements of a trip.

You can't control the weather, but you *can* control the food. If the food is good, people will speak well of the trip, even if the weather was bad.

Everyone looks forward to food, so make it good.

2
"All Natural" Defined

"All natural" is a term fraught with difficulties. Some chemicals, like caffeine, salt, and sugar, occur naturally. Yet too much caffeine, salt, and sugar is not healthy. Meanwhile, some synthetic additives, like vanillin and ascorbic acid, are not harmful and in fact are used by the body as vanilla and Vitamin C would be used. In short, it is not enough to look for products advertised as having "no preservatives" or "no artificial ingredients," because these products may have other "natural" additives that should be avoided.

The Center for Science in the Public Interest (CSPI) is a nonprofit public-interest organization that advocates improved health and nutrition policies. The ratings presented here are from the Center's "Chemical Cuisine" poster[1] and *The Complete Eater's Digest and Nutrition Scoreboard*[2] by Michael F. Jacobson, executive director

---

1. Copyright 1992, Center for Science in the Public Interest. Adapted from *Chemical Cuisine*, which is available from CSPI, 1875 Connecticut Avenue N.W., #300, Washington, D.C. 20009, for $4.95.

2. Copyright 1985, Center for Science in the Public Interest. Adapted from *The Complete Eater's Digest and Nutrition Scoreboard.*

of the CSPI. Generally, I have used the more recent rating. In some cases I have noted differences between the two sources.

To the best of my knowledge, the products reviewed in this book do not contain additives that the Center has rated "caution" or "avoid," with these exceptions: I have included products with salt, hydrogenated vegetable oils, and sugar (in its various forms) without noting their presence. These major ingredients of "junk food" are not usually major ingredients in the foods included in this book. I have not noted where caffeine occurs naturally, because in these instances it is not an additive.

I received for review a few products with red-flag additives. Rather than omitting these foods, I have included them to present a more complete picture of the manufacturer's offerings.

I have noted the presence of sodium aluminum phosphate, a standard ingredient in baking powder that is found in many mixes and baked goods, when sodium aluminum phosphate is listed as an ingredient on the label. *The Complete Eater's Digest and Nutrition Scoreboard* recommends using this additive cautiously. Some brands of baking powder do not contain sodium aluminum phosphate. If you are concerned about this additive, check the fine print on your baking powder container to see if it is present.

Although food manufacturers must list monosodium glutamate (MSG) when the additive itself is used, manufacturers do not have to list MSG when the chemical is present in other additives. The National Organization Mobilized to Stop Glutamate, a nonprofit organization based in Santa Fe, New Mexico, warns that hydrolyzed vegetable protein, autolyzed yeast, and yeast extract contain MSG, and a variety of other additives may contain it as well. In chapters 8 and 9 I have noted when a product contains hydrolyzed vegetable protein, autolyzed yeast, or yeast extract, but I have not identified other additives that possibly contain MSG.

Most companies make available, upon request, ingredient lists and nutritional information for their products. MSG-sensitive individuals would do well to consult these lists as well as keep current on MSG-containing additives. (See Resources at the end of this book.)

Food Additives

According to the Center for Science in the Public Interest, "safe" items are those that appear to cause no harm. Additives marked "caution" are ones that are not well tested, that may not be safe, or that are eaten in excessive quantities. Additives marked "avoid" are ones that are poorly tested or are not safe in the quantities generally eaten.

According to CSPI, dextrose, glucose, corn sugar, corn syrup, and invert sugar—all common additives that are forms of sugar—should be consumed with caution because they provide empty calories. Hydrogenated vegetable oil is safe in small amounts but should be avoided in large quantities. CSPI recommends avoiding both sugar and salt in large amounts.

Additives

Alginate	Safe	
Alpha tocopherol (Vitamin E)	Safe	
Artificial colorings		
Blue no. 1	Avoid	
Blue no. 2	Avoid	
Citrus Red no. 2	Avoid	
Green no. 3	Avoid	
Red no. 3	Avoid	
Red no. 40	Caution	
Yellow no. 5	Caution	*Eater's Digest*: Aspirin-sensitive people should avoid
Yellow no. 6	Avoid	
Artificial flavorings	Caution	
Ascorbic acid (Vitamin C)	Safe	
Aspartame	Caution	*Eater's Digest*: Sensitive people and pregnant women should avoid
Beta carotene	Safe	
Butylated hydroxytoluene (BHT)	Avoid	
Butylated hydroxyanisole (BHA)	Avoid	

(Continued on next page)

Additives *(continued)*

Caffeine	Avoid	*Eater's Digest*: Adults should use with caution; children and pregnant women should avoid
Calcium carbonate	Safe*	
Calcium chloride	Safe*	
Calcium propionate	Safe	
Calcium stearoyl lactylate	Safe	
Calcium sulfate	Safe*	
Caramel color	Safe*	
Carrageenan	Caution	Note: Small amounts probably safe but more testing needed
Casein	Safe	
Citric acid	Safe	
Dicalcium phosphate	Safe*	
EDTA	Safe	
Erythorbic acid	Safe	
Ferrous gluconate	Safe	
Fumaric acid	Safe	
Gelatin	Safe	
Glycerin (glycerol)	Safe	
Gums	Safe	
Hydrogenated vegetable oil	Caution	*Eater's Digest*: Safe in moderate amounts; avoid large amounts
Hydrolyzed vegetable protein (HVP)	Safe	
Lactic acid	Safe	
Lactose	Safe	
Lecithin	Safe	
Mannitol	Safe	
Mono- and diglycerides	Safe	
Mononitrate	Safe*	
Monocalcium phosphate	Safe*	
Monosodium glutamate (MSG)	Caution	
Phosphoric acid; phosphates	Caution	
Polysorbate 60	Safe	
Potassium sorbate	Safe	
Propyl gallate	Avoid	
Propylene glycol alginate	Safe	
Saccharin	Avoid	

(Continued on next page)

Additives *(continued)*

Salt (sodium chloride)	Avoid	Moderate amounts safe but avoid large amounts
Silicon dioxide	Safe*	
Sodium aluminum phosphate	Caution*	
Sodium benzoate	Safe	
Sodium bisulfite	Avoid	*Eater's Digest*: Asthmatics should avoid; others use with caution
Sodium carboxymethylcellulose (CMC)	Safe	
Sodium caseinate	Safe	
Sodium citrate	Safe	
Sodium metabisulphite	Avoid	*Eater's Digest*: Asthmatics should avoid
Sodium nitrite, sodium nitrate	Avoid	
Sodium propionate	Safe	
Sodium stearoyl lactylate	Safe	
Sorbic acid	Safe	
Sorbitan monostearate	Safe	
Sorbitol	Safe	
Starch, modified starch	Safe	
Sugar (sucrose)	Avoid	*Eater's Digest*: Moderate amounts safe, but avoid large amounts
Sulfiting agents	Avoid	*Eater's Digest*: Asthmatics avoid, others use with caution
Sulfur dioxide	Avoid	Asthmatics should avoid
Vanillin, ethyl vanillin	Safe	

*These additives are not included on Chemical Cuisine chart. Ratings are from *The Complete Eater's Digest and Nutrition Scoreboard.*

3
Buying
and Packing
Trail Food

You can find trail food in supermarkets, specialty shops, ethnic markets, health-food stores, and backpacking stores. It may take a bit of detective work, though. I have found food suitable for camping in the prepared-food, ethnic-food, dietetic products, health-food, and general food sections of my local supermarket.

If you are planning anything more than a weekend trip, take a few minutes to do a reconnaissance of your grocery store. Go through the aisles looking for items that appeal to you, that are in your price range, and that you could carry in a pack. Do the same thing if you shop at ethnic- or health-food stores.

Outdoor stores do not usually carry a wide selection. If you are interested in using prepackaged freeze-dried or dehydrated entrees, contact one or more of the companies that make these products and ask for their brochures. If you see items you like in the brochure, you can then either order directly from the company or get your local store to special-order the products for you.

As you plan, jot down your itinerary, your budget, your estimated weight limit, target calories, and other considerations. I find it is helpful to make up a chart with the number of days I will be out and notes about those days. Then, I make lists of what I have in the house, what I have to buy, and anything special I have to do.

Planning a Camping Trip

In the following example, I am planning a backpacking trip in the mountains, so I want to go fairly light. Dinner on Day 1 and breakfast on Day 2 will be near the car, so I can take fresh food in a cooler for those meals. I'll make tabouli, a quick cold salad, for the first night.

From Day 2 lunch through Day 6 breakfast, I've scheduled lightweight food that is moderately economical of fuel. I've planned for two uncooked breakfasts, granola and muesli, so I can get early starts.

Next, I make a list of things to buy and do. "To do" includes making granola, muesli, and tabouli. I already have dried tomatoes, onions, and peppers for the tortellini stew. After I have done the shopping and cooking, I assemble tape, marker, and plastic bags.

To make things easy on trail, I put all items for a meal plus cooking directions in one bag, labeling the bag by meal and day. Because it's just me, I will probably pack the lunch items in bulk rather than per day, to save on plastic bags. (If I were going with a group, though, I would package by day so there would be no chance of running short.)

To decide how much gas to take, I will add up the number of cups of water I'll need for hot drinks, soup, pasta alfredo, instant oatmeal, and cleanup, and factor in fuel for cooking the Spanish rice for 10 minutes, the tortellini stew for 15 minutes, and the wheat pilaf for 15 minutes. I'll include some extra, for cleanup and good measure.

If you are traveling with a group, you have to be thorough about labeling and including directions for each item. *You* may know that the oatmeal should be cooked in three cups of water and that sugar feels different than powdered milk, but the person who does the cooking that morning may not. If I'm using a boxed mix, I tear off the directions and include them in the bag.

There are several ways to organize group food. You can package everything by meal and distribute the parcels in

Notes on Trip to Mountains

	Breakfast	Lunch & Snacks	Dinner
Day 1: Afternoon, drive to trailhead campsite		bag lunch in car: sandwiches and fruit	tabouli bread fruit herb tea
Day 2: Hike to Moose Pond	fried eggs hash browns 2 English muffins fruit tea	bread peanut butter jelly 1 oz cheese 1 c gorp 2 granola bars 1/2 c dried apples	1 c instant soup Spanish rice mix freeze-dried corn 4 fig bars herb tea
Day 3: Day trip from Moose Pond	2 pkts oatmeal with 1/4 c raisins, 1/4 c sunflower seeds, 1/3 c powdered milk bagel & cream cheese tea	bread tahini jerky chocolate apricots mixed nuts	1 c (dry) tortellini with dried vegetables 1/4 c Parmesan cheese 2 brownies herb tea
Day 4: Hike to Black Spruce Mt.	1 c granola with 1/3 c powdered milk bagel & cream cheese tea	same as Day 2	pasta alfredo 2 brownies herb tea
Day 5: Hike over mountain to Cirque Pond	1 c muesli bagel & cream cheese tea	same as Day 3	wheat pilaf mix with 1/4 c cheese, dried veggies 2 coconut bars herb tea
Day 6: Hike out to car mid-morning	2 pkts oatmeal with 1/3 c powdered milk, 1/4 c raisins, 1/4 c cashews, 1 pkt butter tea	1 c gorp 2 granola bars	

(Continued on next page)

Notes on Trip to Mountains *(continued)*

Food I have in the house:	Food I need to buy at the supermarket:	Buy at outdoor store:
oatmeal (granola, muesli)	Spanish rice mix	pasta alfredo dinner
eggs	box of tortellini	freeze-dried corn
tea	3 bagels	
dried veggies	jar of peanuts	
dried apples	box of raisins	*Buy at deli*
cashews	bag chocolate bits	4 brownies
sunflower seeds	bag of apricots	2 coconut bars
Parmesan cheese	2 boxes granola bars	
fig bars	tub of cream cheese	
tomato soup packet	1 bag English muffins	*Make at home*
powdered milk	1 box instant oatmeal	granola
peanut butter	wheat pilaf mix	muesli
jelly	1 chocolate bar	tabouli
walnuts	3 pieces fresh fruit	bag lunch for Day 1
cashews	1 small loaf bread	
tahini		
jerky		
potatoes		

---

whatever manner is fair; you may want to redistribute food during the trip to keep the weight equitable. It is hard, though, when parts of a meal are spread out in several packs: You may be trying to collect dinner while everyone else is busy putting on dry socks. Also, people typically forget what they are carrying, so if you can manage it, keep a list.

Another system is to make up three big bags, one each for breakfast, lunch and snacks, and dinner, then decide daily what you would like to eat. Staples to be used in several meals, such as oil, spices, and extra biscuit mix for baking, can be put in a "pantry" bag.

If you want to share the job of planning and packing, you can take the number of days on trail, divide it by the number of people on the trip, and assign each person individual meals or days. A variation on this theme allows each person to pack his or her own breakfast, lunch, and snacks, plus an assigned number of dinners for the whole group. This method accommodates individuals who have special needs, such as food allergies or a high metabolism.

I have used all of these systems at one time or another. The key is to agree ahead of time on the type of food to be carried and on the approximate number of calories that will be needed per meal. I went hungry on one outing, a combination hiking and canoeing trip, when a friend and I did not communicate well. When she said she'd brought "lots of food" for lunches, I assumed she meant "lots of calories." She actually meant "lots of fresh fruit and vegetables." My jaw dropped when I saw the celery sticks. It's a lesson I haven't forgotten.

Tips for Buying and Packing

Seasonings

Seasonings make the difference between wonderful food and wallpaper paste. On a major trip, I may carry an entire spice kit, including chili and red peppers, cinnamon, curry, garlic cloves or powder, ginger, nutmeg, onion powder, parsley, pepper, salt, thyme, and Italian mix (2 teaspoons parsley, 1 teaspoon oregano, 1 bay leaf, and 1/4 teaspoon each of thyme, rosemary, sage, and garlic). On a shorter trip, I am more likely to measure out the spices and pack them with the ingredients for that dish and carry just a few basic spices in the pantry.

Garlic cloves and ginger root have a much fuller taste than do their powdered forms. If you do use powdered seasonings, at least make sure they are fresh, because spices and herbs lose their potency with time. When you use seasonings, measure them out into your hand rather than pour them from the container into the pot so that you do not add more than you want by mistake.

When storing herbs, do not use old film canisters, which can retain manufacturing chemicals.

Odds and Ends

All-vegetable margarine keeps better than does butter or margarine containing milk solids.

Because it has more fat, whole-milk powder does not keep as well as nonfat milk powder does. In this book, I call for nonfat milk powder. If you use whole-milk powder instead, use 1/4 cup instead of the designated 1/3 cup of nonfat powdered milk. Whole milk does have more calories than the nonfat variety.

If you buy cheese in bulk and want to use it throughout a long trip, package it in the following manner. Cut the block into daily portions, wrap each piece in cheesecloth, and dip it in hot wax. Double-bag with plastic, because if the weather is hot, oil may leak through the cheesecloth. Cheddar cheese prepared this way lasted through one week of very hot weather plus seven weeks of cooler Canadian tundra climate and still tasted good at the end of the trip.

Dehydrating Your Own Food

One fall, when I had overbought pears at a pick-your-own orchard and the fruit was getting ripe all at once, I borrowed a friend's dehydrator. The pears came out so well that I could immediately see the possibilities for trail food.

I received a dehydrator that Christmas, so I skipped the intermediate stages of drying in an oven and building a dryer. My dehydrator, a Harvest Maid, came with five trays and two types of tray liners (one fine screen for moist or extra-small pieces, and one solid tray for liquids and leathers). The unit is efficient and easy to use.

I have dried fruits and vegetables, herbs, and several vegetarian entrees for use on trail. I've also made beef jerky, though I have not dried other meat, chicken, or fish. The key to dehydrating food is to experiment and to keep notes about what you have done.

Although you can get good results from a homemade dryer or even from the oven, if you are going to be processing any amount of food, you should consider buying a dehydrator. Check your local hardware store, appliance store, or outdoor store. I have also seen dehydrators advertised in gardening and mail-order catalogs.

The dehydrator should have a thermostat, which allows you to select the correct drying temperature, and a fan, which makes the unit more energy-efficient and means you have to do less tray-shuffling. Tray liners make it possible to dry entrees, fruit leather, and sauces, and make it much easier to dry high-moisture produce like tomatoes. Some dehydrators are expandable and can handle extra trays. I have found that five trays will hold about all the hand-sliced food I want to prepare at one time, but when I'm using the food processor I could easily fill ten trays.

Your dehydrator should come with a booklet that tells you all you need to know. My standby reference is Harvest Maid's booklet, *The Complete Guide to Food Drying*, which came with my dehydrator.

The Basics of Dehydrating Food

Follow these basic guidelines whether you dry produce in your oven or in a dehydrator.

1. Choose vegetables and fruits that are at the height of their flavor. Remove bruised areas. Peel if you wish; skin has vitamins, but it also lengthens drying time.
2. Slice, dice, shred, or blend, depending on the food and the desired product. It is important to cut food into uniform pieces. Most fruits and vegetables should be dried in 1/4- to 3/8-inch slices.
3. Vegetables like corn, peas, and beans, which have a long cooking time, should be steam-blanched or microwaved to prevent enzymes from continuing to ripen the food after it has dried. Fruits like grapes and blueberries, which have a waxy coating, must be dipped into boiling water for one to two minutes to remove the wax, or the fruit will not dry properly. You can use dips such as pineapple juice or lemon juice to reduce discoloration and lengthen shelf life of fruits and some vegetables, though I have not found it necessary to do so.
4. Set your dehydrator ten degrees higher than you will eventually want it, and turn the appliance on several minutes before you start putting in trays. These two steps compensate for the drop in temperature that occurs when you add food. Remember to reduce the temperature in a few hours.

5. Spread food on the racks or sheets. Slices can touch one another but should not overlap. If you are drying tomato sauce or fruit puree for leather, leave a margin around the edge of the sheet. Dry herbs at 95 to 105 degrees (Fahrenheit), vegetables at 130 degrees, and fruits at 135 degrees; if you mix fruits and vegetables, dry them at 135 degrees. Meat, chicken, and fish must be dried at 145 degrees to prevent the growth of bacteria.

   If food is dried at too high a temperature, the outside will dry but the inside will not (this is called "case hardening"), and the food will eventually spoil.

6. Drying time varies greatly depending on the type of dryer, the number of trays, the thickness of the slices, the humidity, the amount of moisture in the food, and so on. Check food after three or four hours, then check periodically, removing samples from the dryer and letting them cool for a few minutes before you test for dryness.

7. Label dried food and store it in a cool (freezing to 60 degrees), dry, dark place in moisture-proof and insect-proof containers. Glass jars and heat-sealed plastic bags work best. Food stored in plastic bags should be placed in a rigid container. If you want to use metal tins for storage, put food in a plastic bag first. Shelf life depends on the type of food that has been dried and whether it was blanched or pretreated. Dried food will lose color and taste over time; the sooner you use it, the better it will taste.

8. Check the containers for moisture during the first week. If you see moisture on the container, put the food back in the dryer.

9. Rehydrate using one cup of water for every cup of vegetables and, to make stewed fruit, two cups of water for every cup of fruit. Allow ample time for rehydration. Dense foods like peas, corn, green beans, and meat take more time than do thinly sliced foods like tomatoes, shredded carrots, and green peppers. Salt and seasonings slow the rehydration process. You can rehydrate in cold water or, to speed the process, in hot water or as you cook.

I want to add a note of caution regarding rehydration. Make sure that food is totally rehydrated before you serve it, and if you are eating someone else's rehydrated food, check it first. I speak from experience. Several years ago, before I got my dehydrator and learned more about the process, I was happily eating a home-dried but hastily rehydrated entree. I cracked a tooth on a chunk of chicken that was as hard as a rock. Let the eater beware.

Drying Food in an Oven

You can dry small amounts of food in your oven if it has a "warm" setting that goes below 150 degrees Fahrenheit. You'll need an oven thermometer to keep track of the temperature, cookie sheets, and cake cooling racks. Do not use window screening, which may be chemically treated. You can use cookie sheets coated with a nonstick surface for drying tomato paste and other semiliquid foods. When you put the trays in the oven, leave the door open so that moisture can escape. Check regularly for dryness and rotate trays or turn over produce as necessary.

Tips for Drying

This list includes only some of the fruits and vegetables that may be dried for use on trail. I urge you to experiment with others.

Fruits: Pretreatment with a natural dip such as lemon juice preserves color, flavor, and shelf life. Fruit can be cut into rings or slices. Pieces may touch but should not overlap on the tray. Dry at 135 degrees.

Vegetables: Some vegetables need to be blanched to stop enzymatic action; in other cases, steaming is optional. Dry at 130 degrees.

Dry legumes and beans (not green beans, which are a vegetable): Use canned beans or prepare and cook beans per recipe. Spread in a thin layer on a tray with nonstick surface and dry at 140 degrees (assuming there is no meat in the recipe). Dry until brittle.

Preparation and Test for Dryness

Produce	Preparation	Test for dryness
Apples	Pare, core, slice 3/8" thick, pretreat (optional)	Pliable
Apricots	Wash, cut in half, turn "inside out" or cut in quarters, pretreat (optional)	Pliable
Bananas	Slice 1/8" thick, pretreat (optional)	Brittle
Peaches	Pare (optional), slice 3/8" thick, pretreat (optional)	Pliable
Pears	Pare, core, slice 3/8" thick, pretreat (optional)	Pliable
Pineapple	Core, cut 1/4" thick	Pliable
Plums	Wash, remove pit, slice 3/8" thick	Pliable
Beans, green	Wash, cut into 1" pieces, steam until almost done	Brittle
Broccoli	Wash, cut into small pieces, steam 3–5 min.	Brittle
Cabbage	Trim, slice 1/8" thick	Leathery
Carrots	Wash, slice 1/8" thick or grate, do not steam if using immediately; otherwise, steam until tender	Leathery
Celery	Wash, trim, slice 1/4" thick, steam (optional)	Brittle
Corn	Cook corn on cob and remove kernels	Shrunken, dry
Cucumber	Pare, slice 1/8" thick	Leathery
Mushrooms	Clean, slice 3/8" through cap and stem	Leathery
Onions	Trim, slice 1/4"	Brittle
Peas	Shell, steam until almost done	Shrunken, dry
Peppers, green	Wash, trim, slice 1/4" or chop	Leathery
Potatoes (white)	Wash, trim, slice 1/8" thick or dice, steam until almost done	Brittle
Tomatoes	Wash, dip in boiling water to remove skin (optional), slice 3/8" thick	Leathery
Zucchini	Wash, trim; for chips, slice 1/8" thick; otherwise, dice	Leathery

Information from Harvest Maid's *The Complete Guide to Food Dehydrating.*

4
Quick Reference Charts for Buying, Packing, and Cooking

You need five cups of rolled oats, but the store sells oats by the pound. How many pounds do you buy? (The answer: 1 pound.) This is only one of the many questions that may arise as you pack out a trip, whether for yourself or a group. The following charts provide information that can make the process of planning and packing easier.

Abbreviations and Conversion Tables

Abbreviations

t = teaspoon
T = tablespoon
c = cup
lb = pound
oz = ounce
g = gram
fl oz = fluid ounce

Conversion Tables

Can Sizes
No. 1 = 1-1/3 cups
No. 2 = 2-1/4 cups
No. 2-1/2 = 3-1/4 cups
No. 5 = 6-1/2 cups
No. 10 = 13 cups

Conversion Tables *(continued)*

Volume

1 t = 1/3T = 1/6 fluid oz	10-2/3 T = 2/3 c = 5-1/3 fluid oz
3 t = 1 T = 1/2 fluid oz	12 T = 3/4 c = 6 fluid oz
2 T = 1/8 c = 1 fluid oz	14 T = 7/8 c = 7 fluid oz
4 T = 1/4 c = 2 fluid oz	16 T = 1 c = 8 fluid oz
5-1/3 T = 1/3 c = 2-2/3 fluid oz	
8 T = 1/2 c = 4 fluid oz	1 pint = 2 cups
	1 quart = 2 pints

Weight Measures

4 quarts = 1 gallon

1 g = 0.35 oz
1 oz = 28.35 g
1 lb = 16 oz = 453.59 g

Cups to Pounds

One pound	Cups, uncooked,	One pound	Cups, uncooked
Almonds	3-1/3	Couscous	2-2/3
Apples, dried, packed	4 to 5	Dates, dried, pitted,	
Apricots, dried,		loosely packed	2-1/2
loosely packed	3-1/2 to 4	Eggs, powdered	4
Baking mix	4	Falafel, instant,	
Barley	2-1/2	powdered	3-1/4
Barley, quick-cooking	3	Farina (creamed wheat)	3
Beans (small)	2-1/3	Flour, unsifted	3-1/2
Beans (large)	2-1/2 to 2-3/4	Fruit drinks, dried, with sugar	3
Beans, black, instant,		Honey	1-1/3
powdered	4-3/4	Hummus, instant	
Biscuit mix	4	powdered	4
Bulgur	2-1/2	Kasha (roasted buck-	
Cashews	3-1/3	wheat groats)	3-1/3
Cheese, Cheddar,		Lentils	2-2/3
grated	4 to 5-1/3	Macaroni elbows	4
Cheese, Parmesan,		Margarine	2
grated	5-1/3	Milk, noninstant,	
Cheese, powdered	4	powdered	4
Chocolate chips	2-2/3	Milk, instant powdered	6
Cocoa mix	4-1/2 to 6	Millet	2-1/2
Coconut	5 to 6	Molasses	1-1/3
Cornmeal	3-1/4	Noodles, egg	8 to 9

(Continued on next page)

Cups to Pounds *(continued)*

One pound	Cups, uncooked,	One pound	Cups, uncooked
Nut butters	1-2/3	Rice	2-2/3
Oats, quick or regular	5	Rice, creamed	2-1/2
Oats, steel-cut (Scotch)	3	Rice, wild	2-2/3
Oil	2-1/4	Rice, wild, quick	4
Onion flakes	5-1/2	Rotini (pasta spirals)	6
Peaches, dried,		Rye flakes	5
loosely packed	3	Sesame seeds	3-1/4
Peanut butter	1-2/3	Sour cream powder	4
Peanuts	3-1/2	Sugar, white	2-1/3
Peas, split	2-1/4	Sugar, brown, packed	2-1/2 to 3
Pecans	3-1/2	Sunflower seeds	3-1/2
Popcorn	2-1/4	Tahini	1-2/3
Potato flakes	8 to 10-1/2	Tortellini	4
Prunes	2-1/2 to 3	Vegetables, mixed,	
Raisins	2-3/4 to 3	dried	6
Refries, instant,		Walnuts	3-1/2
powdered	3-1/2	Wheat germ	4

Cooking Times and Yields

Approximate cooking time and yields for one cup dry or—for Chinese noodles, angel hair pasta, and spaghetti—for 4 ounces:

Food	Cooking time (minutes)	Cooking water (approx. cups)	Yield (cups)
Barley	35–40	3	3-1/2
Barley, quick	10–12	3	3
Beans, black	Soak +90*	4	2 to 3
Beans, kidney	Soak +60–90*	3	2 to 3
Beans, navy	Soak +90*	3	2 to 3
Bulgur	20	2	2-1/2
Couscous	Add b. water	2	3 to 3-1/2

(Continued on next page)

Food	Cooking time (minutes)	Cook water (approx. cups)	Yield (cups)
Kasha (roasted buckwheat)	10–15	2	3
Lentils	45–60	3	2-1/4 to 3
Macaroni	8–10	large amount**	1-3/4 to 2-1/4
Millet	25–30	2	3-1/2
Noodles, egg	7–10	large amount**	2
Noodles, Chinese (4 oz)	3	large amount**	1-3/4
Oats, rolled, quick	1, let stand 2–3	2	2
Oats, rolled, regular	5 to 15	2	2
Oats, steel-cut	15–20	3-1/3	3-1/2
Pasta, angel hair (4 oz)	3	large amount**	2
Pasta, very small pieces	5	2	1-3/4 to 2
Peas, split	45–60	3	2-1/4
Rice, brown	40	2	3
Rice, brown, quick	10 or less	1-1/3	2
Rice, creamed, quick	30 sec, stand 3 min	4	4
Rice, parboiled	25–30	2	3
Rice, wild	45	4-1/2	3 to 3-3/4
Rice, wild, precooked	7–15	2	2-1/2
Spaghetti (4 oz)	14–18	large amount**	2
Tortellini	20–25	large amount**	2
Wheat, creamed, quick	30 sec	5	5

*To cook beans, check them first, removing small stones and other debris, and then rinse. To reduce flatulence, soak beans for six to eight hours in cold water, or bring beans to boil for two minutes and let stand for one hour. Putting a small amount of baking soda in the soak water also helps leach out sugars that produce gas. Drain liquid and then add beans to fresh water and cook until tender.

**Ideally, the ratio should be one cup pasta to one quart boiling water and one cup Chinese noodles to two quarts boiling water. If this ratio is not possible, use the largest pot available. Pasta should be cooked *al dente*, or still a bit firm. Check by tasting. Pasta should not be mushy.

Rehydration Yields for Instant Mixes

	Use	*Add*	*To make*
Black beans, instant	1 c dry	1 c boiling water	1 c
Falafel, instant	1 c dry	2/3 c cold water	3 small burgers
Hummus, instant	3/4 c dry	3/4 c boiling water	1 c
Potato flakes	3/4 c dry	1 to 1-1/4 c boiling water	1 to 1-1/4 c
Refries, instant	1/2 c dry	1/2 c boiling water	1 c
Tomato powder	1/4 c dry	1 c water	1 c sauce

Approximate Dehydration Yields for Fruits and Vegetables

Use this chart if you are adapting your own recipes for trail use, but remember that the amounts are approximate. The yields depend on the size of the fruit or vegetable, how thin you slice the pieces, how dry they get, and how tightly you pack them in the cup.

	This amount	*Makes approx. this amount dehydrated*
Apple	1 medium sliced	about 7 rings, 3/4 c, or 1.6 oz
Beans, green	1 c	3 T
Carrot, 1 medium	1 c shredded	1/4 c
Carrot, 1 medium	1 c sliced	scant 1/2 c dry
Celery, 2-1/2 large stalks	1 c chopped	1-1/2 to 2 T
Cherries, 16 oz can	1-1/2 c drained	1/2 c loosely packed
Cucumber	1 medium sliced	about 60 chips
Corn	1 c	1/2 c
Mushrooms, 7 medium	1 c sliced	1/4 c
Onion	1 medium	1/3 c
Pear	1 medium sliced	5–7 rings
Peas, green	1 c	scant 1/2 c
Pepper, green, 1 medium	1 c chopped	2-1/2 to 3 T
Pineapple, crushed, 20 oz can	1 c packed, drained	1 c loosely packed
Potato, 1 medium	1-1/3 c diced	1/2 c dried
Potato, 1 medium	sliced	20–25 slices
Spinach	1 c	1/2 c packed
Tomato	1 medium sliced	8–12 chips
Zucchini	1 medium sliced	about 60 chips

5
Cooking on Trail

Assembling a Cook Kit

When you assemble your cooking utensils, think about the recipes you have planned. What is the largest quantity you will be cooking? How many pots will you need at any one meal? Will you need any special utensils, like a small grater or a whisk?

My standard cook set includes:

- two or three nesting pots with lids
- a small pan for frying (most cook sets include a pan)
- pot grippers and/or a pot holder
- plastic spatula
- wood or plastic spoon
- knife
- one bowl, mug, and spoon per person
- one-cup measure (for measuring and for serving)
- pot scrubber and biodegradable soap
- matches, with lighter as a backup
- coffee filters and plastic cone
- baking device
- stove and fuel and/or grill for fire

You might also want to consider taking:

- small whisk
- small grater
- collapsible water jug
- small tea kettle
- pressure cooker

If you are economizing and do not want to take a one-cup measure, then be sure to mark your mug for 1/4-, 1/3-, 1/2-, 2/3-, and 3/4-cup amounts. Many people are now using large insulated mugs on trail. These mugs generally hold 2 cups when filled to the brim; megamugs hold more. If you plan to use ingredients from a pantry, you might also calculate how much your spoon will measure. When leveled, a normal-sized spoon that you would use at the table (not a soup spoon) contains a little more than 1 teaspoon. A heaping spoon contains about 2 tablespoons.

If I am car-camping, I will take a tea kettle or reserve one cooking pot solely for heating water in order to safeguard hot drinks from unidentified small floating things that sometimes appear when a pot has not been thoroughly cleaned.

Fires or a Stove?

Wood fires have gone or are going out of style in many parts of the country, particularly in high mountain areas and areas that get heavy use. In some parks, wood fires are simply not allowed. These trends make sense where wood is not a limitless resource, and where using open fires leads to the degradation of the environment.

Stoves that use oil by-products are not, however, environmentally benign. Gas, butane, and kerosene are non-renewable resources, and pollution is created when oil is drilled for, distilled, and burned.

I have done most of my camping in areas with an abundance of firewood. Sometimes I take a gas stove anyway, because it is more convenient than a wood fire. Often, I don't even make a traditional campfire, for it no longer seems to be a required element of the camping experience. Perhaps I'm a bit lazier than I used to be, and more inclined to crawl into the tent when the bugs are bad.

Whether you rely on wood or gas for fuel should depend on the area in which you are traveling and your own inclinations. If you do opt for fires, gather wood away from the campsite, gather dead wood only, and be moderate in your use of fire. Make fires only in established fire rings or sites. If you must choose a new site, make the fire on bare rock or on mineral soil, not on duff that can catch fire itself. Of course, when it's time to go, make sure the fire is completely doused. If you can put your hand into the ashes, then it is really out. Disperse the remains so that there is no trace that you have been there.

This book does not include a review of gas, butane, kerosene, or multifuel stoves. If you need a stove, talk to your friends, read outdoor catalogs, and survey various models in your local outdoor store. You may want to consider a wood-burning stove (see Resources). Your stove will be an important piece of equipment, so don't hurry your decision.

I do, however, want to mention one unusual stove. Z.Z. Corp makes a line of wood-burning stoves, of which I have used the smallest model, the Sierra. The Sierra is suitable for one or two people. It is equipped with a tiny battery-driven fan to force air up through the sides of the fire-box and into the fire. There is an adjustable draft. The double-walled firebox is small—4 inches in diameter and 2-1/2 inches high—and the entire stove weighs only 15 ounces. It can boil a quart of water in four minutes burning twigs and scrap wood.

There are several advantages to this stove. You don't have to carry gas, which is heavy and inevitably leaks into your pack. There are few moving parts, so there is less chance for breakdown. There is no need to prime the stove. You do not have to calculate ahead how much fuel you will need, because you can pick up wood near each campsite; also, you will not run out of fuel. You can buy and carry some lightweight "fuel sticks" to use in case of emergencies. The impact on the environment is minimal, since the stove uses only twigs. There is no fire scar, and the stove burns so thoroughly that it produces only a quarter-cup of fine ash as residue.

There are some disadvantages. The firebox is so small that you have to feed the fire continually. If your dinner needs to be simmered for twenty minutes, stoking the fire can become tedious. You should use a pot no larger than 5 or 6 inches in diameter and set the stove on a very stable surface. Depending on the length of your trip, you may have to carry extra batteries for the fan. You should have solid fire-starting skills.

For me, the advantages outweigh the disadvantages when I'm by myself or with one other person, when I am using entrees that require little cooking, when I do not anticipate terribly adverse conditions, and when I'm in an area that allows wood fires.

Baking on Trail

There is nothing quite like the smell of freshly baked biscuits, cornbread, or cake on trail. If you have the time and inclination to bake, you will be well rewarded. Both Dutch ovens and reflector bakers, which are traditional devices for baking, require an open fire. Two new devices, the BakePacker and the Outback Oven, can be used on gas stoves.

Dutch Oven

With a Dutch oven, you supply dry heat from above and below. Conventional Dutch ovens, available in cast iron or aluminum, are wide pots or pans with a flat lid. The thick walls help moderate temperature and decrease the chances of burning your cake. If you are careful, however, you can improvise a Dutch oven by using any pot or frying pan with a secure lid.

First, make a bed of coals. Place a few small rocks among the coals to keep the pot or frying pan slightly up off the heat; some Dutch ovens are made with legs for this purpose. Cover the pot and make a small fire, or place hot coals on the lid. Replenish the fire or coals as needed, and don't peek. Raising the lid lets out the hot air and slows cooking. If you check constantly, you can make a cake fall. Baking time is comparable to that of a kitchen oven if the coals are kept hot.

You can also bake in a frying pan with a lid on a gas stove, though it is difficult to keep the food from burning. Turn your stove to its lowest setting and, if necessary, use a heat diffuser. Periodically, rotate the pan so that the heat will be under different areas. Build a small fire of twigs on top of the pot.

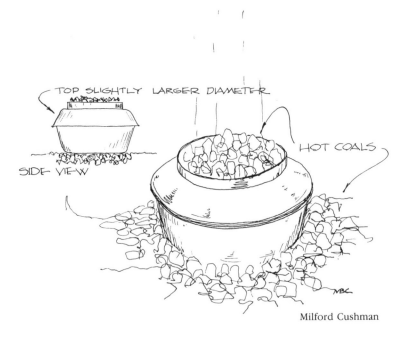

Milford Cushman

Reflector Oven

A reflector oven is an aluminum device that reflects and concentrates heat from a fire. Place the oven about one foot from wood that has been banked outward. The heat of the flames bounces off the two diagonal metal sheets and cooks food evenly, from the top as well as the bottom. Softwood and dry hardwood kindling make good reflector-oven fires.

The oven should be wiped clean after use, since the buildup of soot dulls the surface and decreases the amount of heat that can be reflected. When using a reflector baker, take care not to knock it over. The first time I used one, I stumbled on the corner of the oven and dumped the cake into the fire.

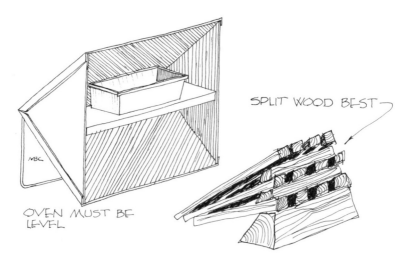

SPLIT WOOD BEST

MBC

OVEN MUST BE LEVEL

Milford Cushman

Improvising a Dutch Oven or a Reflector Oven

Once you master the basics of these methods, you can improvise in any number of ways. On several occasions, when a frying pan but no lid was available, I put several 1-inch-thick sticks in the fire, let them catch on fire, and then placed them across the pan. Some ashes fell onto the cornbread, but I brushed them off when the baking was done.

On another occasion I made an oven by taking the grate off the fireplace, laying the wood along the open end, and banking the fire to burn inward. I pulled embers into the middle of the pit and placed the bread pan on them. The three sides of rock banking reflected heat and the bread baked evenly. When the bread was almost done, I tipped it toward the fire so that it would brown.

I've also made breadsticks, a time-honored method of cooking biscuit dough. Find a smooth stick about 3/4-inch in diameter. Press the dough around the end of the stick and bake the dough over coals. When the biscuit is done, put jelly, honey, or any other filling into the hole. It's fun and delicious.

BakePacker

The BakePacker is a lightweight aluminum grid that works by conducting heat from boiling water up through its aluminum cells and into dough or batter. To bake with this device, place the grid in the bottom of a pot and add enough water to cover the cells. Mix the food ingredients in a sturdy plastic bag (the manufacturer recommends specific bag brands). Place the full bag on the grid and spread the batter over the entire surface of the grid. Keep the plastic away from the sides of the pot and close the bag by loosely folding it down. Cover the pot with a lid. Bring the water to a boil and continue with medium heat for the specified amount of time. Remove the pot from the stove and let it stand for three to five minutes, then

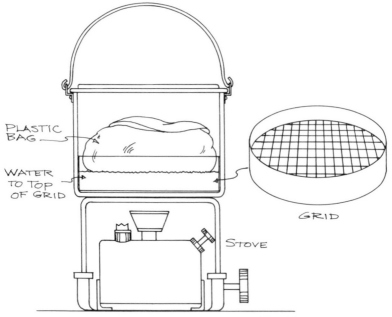

PLASTIC BAG

WATER TO TOP OF GRID

GRID

STOVE

Dawn Peterson

lift out the bread or cake. Tear away the plastic and flip the baked good onto a plate or pot lid. I know it sounds crazy, but it works.

The major drawback to the BakePacker, aside from the fact that you are cooking in plastic, is that because food is steamed, you do not get a golden brown crust. In some cases, such as with biscuits or cornbread, you can compensate by placing the baked goods in a pan and briefly browning them over a gas stove or a fire.

On the other hand, the device is light (8 ounces for the Standard and 4 ounces for the Ultra-Light BakePacker); it is inexpensive (around fourteen dollars for the Ultralight and sixteen dollars for the Standard); it is easy to use; it will not burn food; and it can be used with a gas stove or a wood fire.

You can also cook pancakes, stews, vegetables, grains, and other foods in the BakePacker, the main advantage being that the food will not burn. The BakePacker comes with a booklet of directions and recipes. Adventure Foods sells mixes designed for the BakePacker as well as a cookbook of BakePacker recipes (see Chapter 8 and Resources).

Outback Oven

The Outback Oven turns your gas stove into a little oven. A reflector collar channels heat up into the oven, a diffuser plate with riser bars turns heat from the stove into hot air,

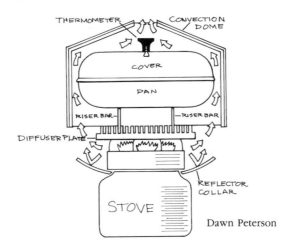

Dawn Peterson

a fiberglass cloth dome holds in the heat, a small vent in the dome lets hot air circulate, and a thermometer on the lid of the baking pan provides a temperature gauge.

The Outback Oven produces outstanding baked goods. It takes some practice to master the technique, however, so it is best to experiment at home, on the back porch. Heat can build up in the oven, so you do have to pay attention to make sure that your food does not burn. You also have to check that all the pieces get back in the bag when you are done. Leaving behind the thermometer or the heat diffuser would cramp your style in the trail kitchen.

But if the Outback Oven requires a bit of attention, it rewards you with wonderful breads and desserts with golden brown crusts that you simply cannot get any other way when you are cooking on a gas stove. The oven can also be used to reconstitute dehydrated or freeze-dried meals.

The Ultralight model, which weighs 9 ounces and sells for about twenty-eight dollars, is a cut-down version designed for backpackers and does not include a baking pan. The Outback Oven Plus Ten, which weighs 28 ounces and sells for about fifty-six dollars, includes a 10-inch Teflon pan that can double as a frying pan. Traveling Light, Inc. carries a line of food mixes for the Outback Oven.

Using a Pressure Cooker

A pressure cooker can decrease cooking time for beans, grains, and legumes by one-third to one-half. If you are using freeze-dried or dehydrated food that cooks quickly, speeding up the process is not necessary. But if you are starting with whole grains or beans, or you are venturing into the high mountains, a pressure cooker can be an invaluable piece of equipment.

I don't know of any pressure cookers that are designed for trail use, so if you are interested in a cooker, check the models in your local hardware and appliance stores. My local stores, for example, have 4- and 6-quart cookers that weigh 5 pounds and cost from thirty to fifty dollars. My own 5-quart cooker, which I bought many years ago, weighs 3 pounds and has two small handles (instead of one large one), making it easier to pack.

When sizing a cooker, choose one that will accommodate the needs of your group. A pressure cooker should be filled no more than halfway when it is used for cooking beans and grains. Pressure cookers typically malfunction when the pot is too full and the steam vent gets clogged.

If you buy a pressure cooker, read and follow the directions carefully and practice with the cooker at home before you use it on trail. For cooking at altitude, increase the cooking time by 5 percent for every thousand feet above 2,000 feet in elevation. In other words, increase the cooking time by 5 percent at 3,000 feet; 15 percent at 5,000 feet; 25 percent at 7,000 feet; 30 percent at 8,000 feet; and so on.

Other Considerations

Cooking at Altitude

As altitude increases, air pressure decreases. And as air pressure decreases, the boiling point of water goes down. At 8,000 feet, water boils at 197 degrees Fahrenheit; at 10,000 feet, it boils at 194 degrees; and at 14,000 feet it boils at 187 degrees.

This change in boiling point means that even though the water is boiling, it is not as hot as it would be at sea level, and therefore does not cook food as quickly. Above 8,000 feet, there is a noticeable difference in cooking times. In fact, for every decrease of 10 degrees, cooking time more or less doubles. It takes twice as long to cook food at 14,000 feet as it does at 8,000 feet.

If you are planning a trip to the high mountains, choose foods that have short cooking times and that require simmering (such as cracked grains) rather than a rolling boil (such as pasta). Although I have spent very little time at altitude, I understand that it is possible to bake up to 10,000 feet without major changes in recipes. You should, however, increase liquid by approximately one tablespoon for every 1,500 feet in elevation gain and lengthen the cooking time somewhat as well.

Water

Gone are the days when you could assume water was safe. With the spread of *Giardia lamblia* (a protozoan that does terrible things to your digestive system) and other organisms, it is imperative to purify the water you use on trail.

There are three methods of purification. You can boil water for three to five minutes (some authorities say ten minutes); you can treat the water with chemicals; or you can use a filter. Most people choose to filter. If you do, make sure that the filter's pore size is small enough to screen out *Giardia* and any other organisms that you might encounter.

Cleanup

Save extra food for leftovers or pack it out with the garbage, but never bury it. Sand and snow work well as pot and bowl cleaners; follow with a rinse of boiling water. If you must use soap, use only a little and make sure it is biodegradable. Do your cleanup well back from lakes and streams, and scatter cleanup water.

Bears

If you are planning on camping in bear country, check with local authorities, such as park rangers, about recommended safety practices. In general, you want to keep food and the smell of food away from your tent site. Set up a separate kitchen area; at night hang your food, toothpaste, and other scented products from a tree or bear pole at some distance from your tent; and keep your clothes and gear free of food odors.

6
Recipes

I devised these recipes so most dishes would be self-contained; that is, you will have all of the ingredients for that dish in one bag. I have, however, assumed that you will be carrying all of your oil or margarine in one separate container. When I say to add 2 tablespoons of oil to the pantry, I mean to add that amount to the separate container you are carrying for the whole trip. If you are using a larger pantry that includes flour, milk powder, baking powder, and so on, then you may want to adjust the recipes.

Check with other people on your trip to make sure that they do not have any food allergies. If they do, consult with them and modify recipes accordingly.

Film canisters work well as small containers for a few teaspoons of an ingredient.

The recipes call for dehydrated vegetables but give the equivalent amount of fresh vegetables in parentheses so that you can substitute if you wish. Onions keep well and are simple enough to chop, so it is almost easier to use fresh than dehydrated onion on the trail.

Sautéing onion in oil sweetens it and adds immeasurably to its taste. You can rehydrate onion and then sauté it, or use a fresh onion. If you are in a hurry or want to simplify a recipe using sautéed onion, you can skip the sautéing.

To rehydrate vegetables, add them to an equal amount of hot water. If you soak thinly sliced vegetables, such as tomatoes, peppers, onions, and shredded carrots, for ten minutes, they will not be fully reconstituted, but they will be edible. Other vegetables, such as potatoes, peas, and mushrooms, should be simmered for ten minutes. Corn, green beans, and celery should be simmered for fifteen to twenty minutes. Use these times as guidelines, not as directives, for there will be some variation. Rehydration time depends on how thin the vegetable was sliced and how much it was dehydrated initially.

Vegetables will rehydrate faster if you soak them in plain water. Rehydration will take longer if you add salt, soup base, or seasonings to the water, or if you add the dried vegetables to a sauce.

To rehydrate fruit, place it in twice as much hot water and let stand for fifteen to thirty minutes. You can speed the process by simmering.

To cook regular brown rice, millet, and bulgur, use two cups of water for every cup of grain. Combine grain and water, bring the water to a boil, and boil without a lid for five minutes. Then simmer with a lid for the remainder of the time. Do not stir, or the grain will become gummy.

For best results, pasta should be cooked *al dente*— slightly firm but not mushy. The only way to tell whether it is done is to test it.

To avoid lumps, always add liquid to powder. Put dry mix in a bowl and slowly add the desired amount of water, stirring constantly. Adding dry mix to a bowl of water will produce lumps.

Throughout this chapter I have called for instant (nonfat) powdered milk. If you are using noninstant powdered milk, use 1/4 rather than 1/3 cup of powder.

I have not called for powdered shortening, honey, or molasses. These ingredients are extremely handy, however, because they are lightweight and you do not have to worry about spilling liquid. (If you would like to use these products, see Chapter 9 for more information.)

Bouillon and soup bases pose a dilemma. I have not yet found tasty bouillon and soup bases that are free of unwanted additives. On the other hand, there may be products in your store with which I am not familiar. Therefore, I am including recipes that call for bouillon or soup base in the hope that you have found—and I may yet find—acceptable products. If you are using a bouillon cube, crush it before adding it to a soup or sauce.

Breakfast

If no one in your party is allergic to milk products, add the powdered milk to the granola or rolled grain when you pack it.

Granola *(make at home)*

17 cups granola plus milk powder
30 to 40 minutes

There are as many granola recipes as there are cooks. I prefer homemade to store-bought granola because the commercial varieties are usually too sweet. Sometimes, on car-camping trips, I'll buy granola and then cut it with another, nonsweetened, cereal. Here is a basic recipe that you can use as is or modify to taste. Dates, coconut, and dried apples are nice variations. Granola is not hard to make—just don't let it burn.

10 c rolled oats
1 c sunflower seeds
1/2 c sesame seeds
1 c chopped almonds
1 c chopped walnuts
3/4 c oil
1/2 c honey
2 c raisins or other dried fruit, chopped
2 c wheat germ
6 c instant milk powder (optional)

At home:
Combine oats, seeds, nuts, oil, and honey in large, flat pan and stir well. Bake at 350 degrees, stirring after 15 or 20 minutes. Continue baking until golden brown, about 30 to 40 minutes total. Remove from oven and stir in dried fruit, wheat germ, and powdered milk. Let cool. Pack in plastic bags.

Nutrition:
Per 1 cup: 607 calories, 27 grams protein, 71 grams carbohydrate, 29 grams fat

Hot Cereal

1 + cup

To shorten cooking time, use quick-cooking grains or put rolled grains through the food processor. Rolled oats, rolled wheat, rolled rye, bulgur, and any combination of rolled grains make excellent hot cereals. You can also add honey, sugar, nuts, sesame seeds, sunflower seeds, margarine, or dried fruit to increase flavor and calories.

At home:
Use 1/2 cup rolled oats or other rolled grain to make 1 cup cereal. (See yields chart, pages 29–30, if using other cooked cereals.) Pack grain, 1/3 cup instant milk powder, and dash salt with other ingredients of your choice.

Hot Cereal Ingredients List

	Amount	Calories	Protein	Carbohydrate	Fat
Almonds	2 scant T	84	3	3	8
Apples, dried	2 rings	31	Tr	8	Tr
Apricots, dried	5 halves	70	1	18	0
Bulgur	1/2 c dry	227	8	47	1
Honey	1 T	65	Tr	17	0
Margarine	1 T	100	Tr	Tr	12
Milk, instant	1/3 c	82	8	12	Tr
Oats, rolled	1/2 c	150	8	27	3
Raisins	2 T	60	Tr	16	Tr
Sesame seeds	2 T	106	3	5	9
Sugar, brown	1 T	40	0	11	0
Sunflower seeds	2 T	83	3	4	7
Walnuts	2 scant T	90	3	2	9

On trail:
Add ingredients to 1 cup boiling water (use slightly more water if dried fruit is added). Cook until done (time depends on type of grain used—see pages 29–30).

Creamy Rice Cereal with Dates and Almonds

2-1/2 cups
Cook 30 seconds; let stand 3 minutes

Even people who dislike hot cereal have liked this recipe. You can use sliced almonds and chopped dates, but chopping the nuts and dates as fine as possible gives the dish a smoother texture. The dates sweeten the cereal, so try it first before you add sugar or honey.

1/2 c creamed rice, quick-cooking
1/3 c almonds, chopped very fine
6 dates, sliced very thin
2/3 c instant powdered milk
dash salt (optional)

At home:
Combine ingredients and place in reclosable plastic bag.

On trail:
Add ingredients to 2 cups boiling water; cook for 30 seconds, stirring; cover and let stand 3 minutes.

Nutrition:
Per 1-1/4 cup: 442 calories, 16 grams protein, 70 grams carbohydrate, 13 grams fat

Toasted Oatmeal

2 cups
Cook 1 minute

If you can't stand another bowl of oatmeal, try this recipe.

1 c rolled oats, quick-cooking
2 t oil
4 t tamari

At home:
Brown oats lightly in oil; add tamari. Put in reclosable plastic bag.

On trail:
Add mixture to two cups boiling water. Stir 1 minute while oatmeal cooks.

Nutrition:
Per 1 cup cooked cereal: 171 calories, 8 grams protein, 27 grams carbohydrate, 6 grams fat

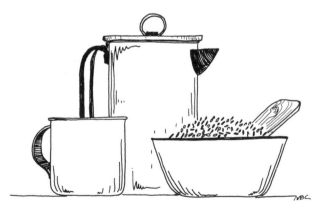

Milford Cushman

Muesli

7-1/2 cups
Let stand 30 minutes or overnight

Muesli is a tasty, easy breakfast. You can make it up the night before and let it stand, allowing the flavors to mix, or—using quick oats—skip the soak and add water in the morning. Muesli is also an excellent breakfast to eat at home and can be made with yogurt and fruit juice instead of milk.

3 c rolled grain, quick-cooking or regular
1/4 c sunflower seeds
1/4 c almonds or other nuts
1/2 c raisins
1/2 c dried apricots or other fruit
2 t cinnamon
2 c instant milk powder
1/2 t salt

At home:
Mix ingredients and place in plastic bag.

On trail:
Add 5 cups water to dry mix; mixture will be soupy. Let soak overnight or, if using quick oats, let stand 30 minutes.

Nutrition:
Per 1-1/4 cup: 358 calories, 18 grams protein, 55 grams carbohydrate, 9 grams fat

Fried Bulgur

5 cups
Soak overnight; fry about 10 minutes

Fried bulgur provides a change of pace for breakfast. I use a fresh onion because it is as easy as rehydrating dried onion.

2 c bulgur, uncooked
1/3 c dehydrated onion or 1 fresh onion
about 1/4 c oil
1-1/3 c grated Cheddar cheese
salt, pepper, garlic powder to taste

At home:
Add 1/2 cup oil to the pantry. Bag bulgur and dehydrated onion (if not using fresh). Grate cheese and place in separate bag.

On trail:
Soak the bulgur (and dehydrated onion) overnight in 4 cups water. Next morning, drain extra water, if necessary. Dice and sauté onion, if using fresh. Add bulgur mixture to skillet and fry until golden brown and crispy, adding salt, pepper, and garlic powder to taste. Fold in grated cheese just before you serve.

Nutrition:
Per 1-1/4 cup serving: 486 calories, 16 grams protein, 53 grams carbohydrate, 24 grams fat

Spiced Fruit Rice Pudding

This recipe is listed with the desserts, but it makes a delicious breakfast. See page 112.

Scrambled Eggs

Dehydrated egg mixtures vary, but usually 2 tablespoons of egg powder equals one medium fresh egg. To make the equivalent of two scrambled eggs, follow the directions on the package or use this recipe. Biscuits are good with scrambled eggs.

4 T egg powder
salt and pepper to taste
about 2 t oil

At home:
Bag egg powder. Add 2 teaspoons oil to pantry.

On trail:
Mix egg powder and 1/3 cup water; fry in oil. Season to taste.

Nutrition:
For 2-egg portion: 123 calories, 3 grams protein, 2 grams carbohydrate, 13 grams fat

Mexican Eggs

1 T dehydrated onion
1 T dehydrated green pepper
1 T tomato powder
garlic powder, chili powder to taste

Rehydrate onion and green pepper in 3 tablespoons hot water for 10 minutes. Combine onion, pepper, tomato powder, and seasonings, then fold into basic egg mixture.

Cheesy Eggs

Add 2 tablespoons grated cheese to basic egg mixture.

Pancakes

On trail:
Add 1/2 cup water per 1 cup Biscuit Mix (page 92). Optional: add 2 tablespoons powdered eggs. Cook in well-oiled pan or in BakePacker. 1 cup Biscuit Mix makes 6 pancakes.

Nutrition:
Per 6 pancakes: 576 calories, 18 grams protein, 93 grams carbohydrate, 16 grams fat

Orange-Poppyseed Pancakes

For a gourmet breakfast, add 1 tablespoon poppy seeds and 1–2 teaspoons orange rind, orange extract, or orange flavoring per 1 cup Biscuit Mix.

Syrup

If you live in New England and you are partial to maple syrup, as I am, then it's worth carrying the real thing. Double-bag the syrup container or carry maple granules that can be rehydrated. You can also make a simple non-maple syrup with one part water, two parts brown sugar or honey, and one part margarine. Or, you can top pancakes with rehydrated apples cooked with cinnamon and a dash of sweetener, or spread on your favorite jam.

Lunch and Snacks

Lunch can be put together from a grab bag of options. Choose foods that you like and that fit the type of trip you are planning. If you are taking fresh food, use it first because it is heavier and may get moldy. Bread, tortillas, and pita bread can last several days, depending on the temperature.

Sometimes I don't stop for lunch, but snack throughout the day. On the Moise and Harricanaw trips (see Chapter 11), a midmorning snack quickly became part of our routine.

The following lunch chart includes nutritional information for a variety of lunch items. How much you take depends on how much you eat, what type of trip you are planning, and what percentage of your calories you want from lunch and snacks. If there are foods you don't see here, check Chapter 7.

Lunch Items

	Amount	Calories	Protein	Carbohydrate	Fat
Almond butter	1 T	101	2	3	10
Apple	1	70	Tr	18	Tr
Apple, dried	5 rings	78	Tr	21	Tr
Apricots, dried	5 halves	70	1	18	Tr
Bagel	1	165	6	30	2
Bannock	3 pieces	288	9	47	8
Black bean					
spread *(mix)*	1/2 c	136	8	23	1
Bread	1 slice	65	3	14	1
Candy, hard	1 oz	110	0	28	Tr
Cheese, Cheddar	1 oz	115	7	1	9
Cheese, Parmesan	1 oz	110	11	1	7
Chocolate, milk	1 oz	145	2	16	9
Couscous salad					
(mix)	1/2 c	103	2	13	5

(Continued on next page)

Lunch Items *(continued)*

	Amount	Calories	Protein	Carbohydrate	Fat
Crackers, rye					
wafers	4 wafers	90	4	20	Tr
Crackers, sea					
rounds	2 crackers	120	2	10	4
Fig bars	2	100	2	22	2
Flapjacks	1 piece	454	9	55	26
Gorp 1	1/2 c	288	8	30	18
Gorp 2	1/2 c	365	9	36	24
Granola bars, oat					
and honey	2 bars	240	4	34	10
Hummus (mix)	1/2 c	111	4	10	7
Jam	1 T	55	Tr	14	Tr
Jerky, beef	1 oz	43	8	0	1
Logan bread	1 piece	629	11	75	38
Mixed nuts	1/2 c	390	14	15	34
Orange	1	65	1	16	Tr
Peaches, dried	5 halves	156	3	40	Tr
Peanut butter	1 T	95	4	3	8
Peanut butter and					
honey spread	1 T	80	2	10	4
Pears, dried	5 halves	230	2	61	Tr
Pita bread	1 piece	106	4	21	1
Prunes	4	70	1	18	Tr
Raisins	1/2 c	240	2	64	Tr
Refries (mix)	1/2 c	136	8	23	1
Salami	1 oz	130	7	Tr	11
Sardines	3 oz	175	20	0	9
Soybeans, roasted	1/2 c	392	29	17	26
Tabouli (mix)	1/2 c	161	2	17	10
Tahini	1 T	89	3	3	8
Tortillas, flour	1	85	3	15	2

Logan Bread *(make at home)*

20 large pieces
Bake 45 minutes

This bread is extremely rich. It is excellent for winter camping because the oil prevents it from freezing hard, as other breads do.

3 c whole wheat flour
3 c unbleached white flour
2-1/2 c rolled oats
1-1/2 c brown sugar
1 c honey
1/2 c molasses
1/2 c powdered milk
6 eggs
1-1/4 c nuts
2 c raisins
3 t baking powder
2 t salt
2 c margarine
1 c oil

At home:
Combine ingredients and stir well. Pour into four 9-by-9-inch greased cake pans and bake at 350 degrees for 45 minutes or until done. After bread has cooled, slice it and store it in the refrigerator or freezer.

Nutrition:
Per piece: 629 calories, 11 grams protein, 75 grams carbohydrate, 38 grams fat

Flapjacks, or Golden Bricks of the North—the original granola bars! *(make at home)*

20 large squares
Bake 20 minutes

Flapjacks were regular fare during my days at Minnesota (now Voyageur) Outward Bound in the early 1970s. At another program, my students called them Golden Bricks of the North. The original recipe, from Britain, called for "golden syrup." The closest substitute I have found is corn syrup. With their base of oats, nuts, and sweetener, flapjacks were the forerunners of granola bars.

9-1/2 c rolled oats
1 c peanuts or almonds
2 c white sugar
2 c margarine
1/3 c honey
1/3 c corn syrup

At home:
Combine ingredients and put into four 9-by-9-inch, well-greased cake pans (or comparably sized cookie sheets with raised edges), pressing dough into a compact layer. Bake at 350 degrees for 20 minutes or until golden brown. Remove from oven and cut into squares, but do not remove the squares from the pan until they have cooled. Store in plastic bags. To protect flapjacks from being crushed and crumbled in your pack, stack them in clean plastic-lined milk cartons.

Nutrition:
Per square: 454 calories, 9 grams protein, 55 grams carbohydrate, 26 grams fat

Peanut Butter and Honey Spread

1 cup

You can take these two ingredients separately, but it is handy to have them already mixed together.

1/2 c peanut butter
1/2 c honey

At home:
Mix well and put in plastic tube or other container.

Nutrition:
Per 1 tablespoon spread: 80 calories, 2 grams protein, 10 grams carbohydrate, 4 grams fat

Milford Cushman

Gorp: Good Old Raisins and Peanuts

5 cups

Gorp has as many recipes as granola does. You can mix various nuts and seeds, dried fruit, and chocolate in whatever combination suits your taste.

Gorp 1 (without chocolate)

1 c peanuts
1 c walnuts
1 c raisins
1 c coconut
1 c chopped dried fruit

At home:
Mix ingredients and bag.

Nutrition:
Per 1/2 cup: 288 calories, 8 grams protein, 30 grams carbohydrate, 18 grams fat

Gorp 2 (with chocolate)

1 c peanuts
1 c walnuts
1 c raisins
1 c chocolate bits

Nutrition:
Per 1/2 cup: 365 calories, 9 grams protein, 36 grams carbohydrate, 24 grams fat

Roasted Soybeans

2 cups

Roasted soybeans have a delicious nutlike flavor. You can roast your own or you may be able to find them at your local health-food store. My home-roasted soybeans have never achieved the peanutlike consistency that store-bought ones have.

2 c soybeans
3 T oil
salt or tamari

At home:
Add 2 cups soybeans to 7 cups water, bring to boil, and boil for 2 minutes. Cover pot and let stand 1 hour. Drain liquid. Add 6 cups water and let soybeans soak for 24 hours; add more liquid if necessary. Spread beans on a cookie tray, preferably a tray with raised edges. Dribble about 3 tablespoons oil and sprinkle salt or tamari over the beans. Bake at 300 to 350 degrees 1 to 2 hours, until the beans are no longer soft, but be careful not to overbake.

Nutrition:
Per 1/2 cup: 392 calories, 29 grams protein, 17 grams carbohydrate, 26 grams fat

Mixed Nuts

4 cups

1 c peanuts
1 c cashews
1 c sunflower seeds
1 c almonds

At home:
Mix and bag ingredients.

Nutrition:
Per 1/2 cup: 390 calories, 14 grams protein, 15 grams carbohydrate, 34 grams fat

Bean Spreads

Refries, hummus, and black bean mixes are available in supermarkets and health-food stores. Some health-food stores even sell the mixes in bulk, by the pound. Refries and black bean spread require boiling water, so they should be rehydrated at breakfast when the stove is going. Hummus requires only cold water, so it can be mixed up at lunch. Hummus is good on crackers or with tahini and/or fresh vegetables in a pita pocket. Refries and black beans are good with salsa and cheese on tortillas.

Salad Mixes

There are several commercial couscous and tabouli salads that can be rehydrated at breakfast (because they require hot water) and served at lunch. These salad mixes are good with pita bread or crackers.

Beef Jerky

4 ounces

1 lb lean flank or round steak
2 T soy sauce
1 T Worcestershire sauce
1 clove garlic, crushed
1/4 t salt

Buy lean meat and trim all fat. Place meat in a freezer and let it freeze partially; it will be easier to slice this way. Slice into 3/8- to 1/4-inch strips and place in marinade. Marinate 12 to 24 hours. Drain liquid and pat strips dry. Place on racks and dry at 145 degrees. The length of drying time will vary according to how thick the slices are: very thin slices may dry in 5 or 6 hours; thicker slices may take 8 to 10 hours or more. One pound of meat makes about 4 ounces of jerky; the actual number of pieces will vary according to size.

Nutrition:
For 1 ounce jerky: 243 calories, 8 grams protein, 0 grams carbohydrate, 1 gram fat

Dinner

Grains and pasta are the bases for most trail dinners. You can expand the possibilities by using potato flakes, dehydrated potatoes, and freeze-dried or dehydrated beans. To compare cooking times, see the cooking times and yields chart on pages 29–30. See also the sauces section, beginning page 98, for what to serve over the carbohydrate. Most of the soups presented here can be used as entrees. The Quick Vegetable and Onion soups, which are both low in calories, can be served before the main dish.

There are many other dinner options, but the basic ingredients and sauces below will give you an idea where to start.

Dinner Ingredients

	Approx. amount cooked	Calories	Protein (grams)	Carbohydrate (grams)	Fat (grams)
Barley	1-1/2 c	255	8	54	2
Beans, refried	1 c	228	14	38	2
Bulgur	1-1/4 c	227	8	47	1
Cheese, Cheddar	1/3 c grated	115	7	1	9
Cheese, Parmesan	1/3 c grated	110	11	1	7
Cheese sauce	1/2 c	340	16	18	26
Chicken, canned	3 oz	170	18	0	10
Couscous (approx. values)	1-1/2 c	300	6	40	15
Curry sauce	1/2 c	219	3	15	18
Gado-gado sauce	1/2 c	211	11	9	16
Kasha	1-1/2 c	290	6	60	0
Lentils	1-1/4 to 1-1/2	310	22	52	2
Macaroni	1-1/2 c	315	11	63	2
Millet	1-1/4 c	216	7	48	2
Noodles	1-1/2 c	330	11	60	5
Potatoes, mashed	1 c	140	4	32	0
Rice, brown	1-1/2 c	232	5	50	1
Spaghetti	1-1/2 c	315	11	63	2
Tomato sauce	1/2 c	88	4	20	Tr
Tuna, canned	3 oz	116	23	0	2

Spaghetti with Pesto or Tomato Sauce

3-1/2 to 4 cups
Cook about 15 minutes

For a quicker meal, substitute angel hair spaghetti, which cooks in 3 minutes.

6 oz thin spaghetti
1/3 c Parmesan cheese
Pesto (page 107) or Tomato Sauce (page 98)

At home:
Break spaghetti into 6-inch pieces and bag. Note cooking time from original package.

On trail:
Add spaghetti to 2 quarts boiling water and stir until water returns to a boil. Cook per instructions, about 15 minutes. Serve with sauce and top with cheese.

Nutrition:
Per 1-1/2 cup pasta and 1/2 cup tomato sauce: 458 calories, 21 grams protein, 84 grams carbohydrate, 6 grams fat; per 1-1/2 cup pasta plus 1/4 cup pesto: 514 calories, 23 grams protein, 66 grams carbohydrate, 27 grams fat

Clam Spaghetti

4 cups
Cook about 15 minutes

I have generally avoided calling for canned products, but clam sauce rounds out a bowl of spaghetti so nicely that I have made an exception for it. Serve this dish the first night out so you do not have to carry the heavy cans too far. I like a hearty sauce, so I use one can of clams and one of sauce. You may opt for just the sauce.

6 oz thin spaghetti
1/3 c Parmesan cheese
1 10-oz can clam sauce
1 10-oz can whole small clams

At home:
Bag spaghetti and cheese separately.

On trail:
Drain water from clams. Cook and drain spaghetti. Add clams and sauce to spaghetti; stir well. Serve with cheese.

Nutrition:
Per 2 cups: 545 calories, 50 grams protein, 47 grams carbohydrate, 18 grams fat

Tortellini

4 cups
Cook 25 to 30 minutes

Tortellini is a small prepared pasta filled with cheese. Dried-spinach or multivegetable tortellini is a simple and filling meal. You can top it with Parmesan cheese, Tomato Sauce (page 98) and cheese, or Pesto (page 107).

2 c tortellini, uncooked
1/3 c grated Parmesan cheese

At home:
Bag tortellini and cheese separately.

On trail:
Add tortellini to 2 quarts boiling water and stir until water returns to a boil. Cook uncovered for 20 to 25 minutes, stirring occasionally. Drain. Serve with cheese.

Nutrition:
Approximate values per 2 cups: 290 calories, 17 grams protein, 40 grams carbohydrate, 6 grams fat

Tortellini Stew

5 cups
Cook 25 to 30 minutes

I made this dish on a winter trip when we arrived at our cabin just as dark fell. The recipe was so popular that night that I've used it again and again, adding whatever dried vegetables I have on hand. The cooking water becomes a tasty broth that can help you rehydrate after a long day.

2 c dried tortellini
20 slices tomato, dehydrated
3 T dehydrated green pepper
1/3 c dehydrated scallions or onions
1 T mixed basil, oregano, and thyme
1/4 c tomato powder (optional)
1/4 t powdered garlic
salt to taste
1/3 c grated Parmesan cheese

At home:
Bag cheese separately. Bag all other ingredients together.

On trail:
Add tortellini mixture to 2 quarts boiling water and stir until water returns to a boil. Cook uncovered for 20 to 25 minutes, stirring occasionally. Serve with cheese.

Nutrition:
Per 2-1/2 cups: 328 calories, 16 grams protein, 57 grams carbohydrate, 5 grams fat

Hot or Cold Rotini Casserole

7 cups
Cook 15 minutes

This colorful dish can be served hot or cold; it is especially nice when made with fresh vegetables. For cold salad, allow the rotini to cool before folding in the other ingredients.

3 c rotini (8 oz)
20 slices tomato, dehydrated (2 medium tomatoes)
3 T dehydrated green pepper (1 medium pepper)
1/3 c dehydrated scallions or onions (2 scallions
or 1 onion)
1 c grated Cheddar cheese
1/3 c Italian salad dressing (a brand that does not
need refrigeration)
salt and pepper to taste

At home:
Bag rotini, vegetables, and cheese separately. Put salad dressing in a leak-proof container and then double-bag for safety.

On trail:
Add rotini and dried vegetables to 2 quarts boiling water, stir until water returns to a boil, and cook 10 to 12 minutes. Drain liquid. If using fresh vegetables, chop them and fold into drained pasta. Add Cheddar cheese and salad dressing, stir well.

Nutrition:
Per 2-1/3 cup: 412 calories, 14 grams protein, 38 grams carbohydrate, 34 grams fat

Macaroni and Cheese

About 4 cups
Cook 8 to 10 minutes plus prepare Cheese Sauce

2 c macaroni
Cheese Sauce (page 100)

At home:
Bag macaroni. Prepare Cheese Sauce ingredients.

On trail:
Cook macaroni in 1 quart boiling water for 8 to 10 minutes, drain. Prepare Cheese Sauce. Serve sauce over macaroni.

Nutrition:
Per 2 cups: 1,100 calories, 43 grams protein, 120 grams carbohydrate, 54 grams fat

One-Pot Mac and Cheese

4 + cups
Cook 12 minutes

2 c macaroni
1 T flour
1/3 c instant powdered milk
1/2 c grated Cheddar cheese
salt and pepper to taste

At home:
Bag macaroni, flour and milk, and cheese separately.

On trail:
Cook macaroni in 1 quart boiling water for 8 to 10 minutes. Drain all but about 3/4 cup water. Stir in flour, milk, and cheese, mixing well.

Nutrition:
Per 2 cups: 561 calories, 26 grams protein, 94 grams carbohydrate, 9 grams fat

Trail Chili

About 6 cups
Cooking time depends on grain

This dish is good with a sprinkling of sharp Cheddar cheese. If you want to boost the calorie count, add a tablespoon or two of margarine.

2 c bulgur, rice, or lentils
Chili Sauce (page 106)

At home:
Bag bulgur, rice, or lentils. Bag Chili Sauce ingredients.

On trail:
Put bulgur, rice, or lentils in 4 cups water, bring to boil, and simmer for 20 minutes (bulgur), 40 minutes (brown rice), 8 to 10 minutes (instant brown rice), or 45 minutes (lentils). Serve with Chili Sauce.

For a one-pot meal, rehydrate onion per Chili Sauce recipe. Sauté onion and seasonings, then add grain or lentils, dried vegetables, and 5 cups water. Bring to a boil and simmer for indicated amount of time. Add more water if necessary.

Nutrition:
Per 2 cups bulgur chili: 375 calories, 13 grams protein, 79 grams carbohydrate, 1 gram fat; per 2 cups rice chili: 381 calories, 9 grams protein, 83 grams carbohydrate, 1 gram fat; per 2 cups lentil chili: 485 calories, 32 grams protein, 85 grams carbohydrate, 1 gram fat

Burritos

8 burritos
Let stand 10 minutes

You can use store-bought tortillas or make them on trail (see page 93).

1-3/4 c instant refried beans mix
8 tortillas
1 c (3 oz) grated Cheddar cheese
1/4 c dehydrated salsa (page 108)

At home:
Bag each ingredient separately.

On trail:
Place salsa in insulated mug, if available. Add 1/2 cup boiling water, cover, let stand 10 minutes, then drain. Add 2 cups boiling water to refries, stir well, cover, and let stand 5 minutes. Warm tortillas in pot lid but do not let them dry out. Roll refries, cheese, and salsa in tortillas.

Nutrition:
Per 4 burritos: 823 calories, 41 grams protein, 115 grams carbohydrate, 24 grams fat

Quesadillas

8 quesadillas
Let stand 10 minutes; cook 15 minutes

Quesadillas are tortilla turnovers. Fill them with cheese, or cheese and vegetables, for a change from one-pot meals.

8 tortillas
6 oz grated or sliced Cheddar cheese
1/2 c dehydrated onion, green pepper, tomato,
  and/or mushrooms (optional)
chili pepper to taste
2 T oil

At home:
Add 2 tablespoons oil to pantry. Bag tortillas, cheese, and dried vegetables separately.

On trail:
Add 1 cup hot water to vegetables and simmer for 10 minutes; drain. Sprinkle half of the tortilla with cheese and vegetables; fold over. Place quesadilla in pan, covered, and heat until cheese has nearly melted. Turn over to brown other side. Use enough oil to keep quesadilla from sticking.

Nutrition:
Per 4 quesadillas (with vegetables): 823 calories, 39 grams protein, 67 grams carbohydrate, 50 grams fat

Black Beans and Rice with Tortilla Chips

6-1/2 cups
Cook 40 minutes

2 c instant black beans
1 c brown rice
3/4 t powdered garlic
1 T chili powder
1/2 t dry mustard
1/2 t ground cumin
1/3 c dehydrated onion (1 medium onion)
1/2 c dehydrated corn or 1 c freeze-dried corn
salt and pepper to taste
1 c grated Cheddar cheese
1 c broken tortilla chips

At home:
Bag cheese and chips separately. Bag remaining ingredients. The chips are for flavor and texture, so don't worry about them getting crushed.

On trail:
Add bean mixture to 5-1/2 cups boiling water, stirring while the water comes to a boil again. Simmer for 40 minutes, stirring occasionally. Serve with cheese and broken tortilla chips.

For a quicker dish, use freeze-dried corn and substitute quick-cooking for regular rice, cooking for 10 minutes.

Nutrition:
Per 2 + cups: 950 calories, 44 grams protein, 139 grams carbohydrate, 26 grams fat

Lentil Stew

About 3-1/2 cups
Cook 25 minutes; let stand 15 minutes

This stew is good with a sprinkling of cheese, if you have some left over from lunch. Decorticated lentils, also called dal, cook more quickly than the type usually found in stores. If you buy dal, adjust the cooking time according to package directions. Add margarine to increase the calorie count.

1 c lentils
3 T dehydrated onion
3 T dehydrated carrot
8 slices dehydrated tomato
10 slices dehydrated potato
2 T tomato powder (optional)
1/4 t salt
1/8 t garlic powder
1/8 t black pepper
1/4 t cumin

At home:
Bag lentils and dehydrated vegetables. Put seasonings in film canister.

On trail:
Add lentils and vegetables to 2-1/3 cups water. Bring to boil, cook for 5 minutes, and then let stand, covered, for 15 minutes. Add seasonings, bring to a boil a second time, and simmer for 20 minutes or until lentils are done. If you have plenty of fuel, leave the lentils on the stove the whole time, about 40 minutes; add seasonings after 20 minutes.

Nutrition:
Per 1-3/4 cups: 417 calories, 24 grams protein, 65 grams carbohydrate, 2 grams fat

Split Pea Stew

3 + cups
Cook 25 minutes; let stand 15 minutes

Follow directions for Lentil Stew, except substitute split peas for lentils and omit dehydrated tomato, tomato powder, and cumin.

Nutrition:
Per 1-1/2 + cups: 395 calories, 23 grams protein, 60 grams carbohydrate, 2 grams fat

Curried Rice

4 cups
Cook 10 or 40 minutes, plus prepare sauce

1 c brown rice
Quick Curry Sauce (page 104)
1/4 c raisins
1/4 c coconut
1/4 c cashews
1/4 c peanuts

At home:
Bag rice. Bag Quick Curry Sauce ingredients. Bag other ingredients.

On trail:
Cook rice in 2 cups water for 40 minutes (regular rice) or 10 minutes (quick-cooking). Make sauce. Serve rice with sauce and raisin-nut mixture.

Nutrition:
Per 2 cups: 773 calories, 17 grams protein, 95 grams carbohydrate, 40 grams fat

Alpine Rice

6 + cups
Cook 10 or 40 minutes

2 c brown rice
2 T margarine
1/3 c grated Parmesan cheese
1/3 c grated Muenster cheese
2 T instant powdered milk
1/4 c sesame seeds
salt to taste

At home:

Add 2 tablespoons margarine to pantry. Bag rice. Bag cheeses and powdered milk together. Sauté sesame seeds in 1 tablespoon oil until browned, let cool, and bag separately.

On trail:

Cook rice 40 minutes (regular) or 10 minutes (quick-cooking). Add remaining ingredients plus 1/2 cup hot water; mix well. Sprinkle with sesame seeds. Serve at once.

Nutrition:

Per 2 + cups: 527 calories, 16 grams protein, 74 grams carbohydrate, 18 grams fat

Risi E Bisi

About 8 cups
Cook 10 or 40 minutes

2 c brown rice
1 c dehydrated or 2 c freeze-dried peas
1/3 c dehydrated onion
2 T oil
2/3 c Parmesan cheese
tamari or salt to taste

At home:
Add 2 tablespoons oil to pantry. Bag rice and peas. Bag onion.

On trail:
Simmer onion in 1/3 cup hot water for 10 minutes, drain, and sauté in oil. Add rice, peas, and 5 cups water; cook for 40 minutes (regular rice) or 10 minutes (quick-cooking), or until peas are fully rehydrated. Sprinkle with cheese and serve.

Nutrition:
Per 2 + cups: 414 calories, 15 grams protein, 62 grams carbohydrate, 12 grams fat

Fried Bulgur

This recipe is in the breakfast section (page 51), but if you can't face garlic and cheese that early in the day, then have it for dinner.

Variations: For Bulgur with Vegetables, put uncooked bulgur, 1 cup dehydrated vegetables, and 5 cups water in a pot. Bring to boil, cover, and let stand 20 minutes. Simmer if more cooking is needed. Serve as is with cheese, or fry until crispy and then add cheese.

For Toasted Wheat and Celery au Gratin, use 1/2 cup dehydrated celery, 1/2 teaspoon celery seed, and 1/3 cup dehydrated onion instead of mixed vegetables.

Cheesy Potatoes

About 4 cups
Cook 10 minutes, and prepare sauce

80 to 100 dehydrated potato slices (approximately 4 potatoes)
Cheese Sauce (page 100)

At home:
Bag potatoes and Cheese Sauce ingredients separately.

On trail:
Add potatoes to 2 quarts boiling water and cook for 10 minutes or until potatoes are done; drain. Meanwhile, make Cheese Sauce. Serve over potatoes. For quick cheesy potatoes, cook potatoes and sprinkle with 1 cup grated cheese. Season with your favorite seasoning.

Nutrition:
Per 2 cups: 860 calories, 38 grams protein, 78 grams carbohydrate, 52 grams fat

Shepherd's Pie

4 + cups
Cook 10 minutes, plus prepare sauce

1-1/2 c potato flakes
White Sauce (page 99) made with Worcestershire
sauce
1 3-oz can chicken
1/2 c dehydrated vegetables or 1 c freeze-dried
vegetables

At home:
Bag potato flakes and dehydrated vegetables separately.
Prepare White Sauce ingredients.

On trail:
In pot lid, simmer vegetables in 1 cup (or more) water until
they are rehydrated, about 10 minutes for any vegetable
except corn, which requires 20 minutes. Boil 1-1/4 cup
water in pot and add potato flakes, stirring quickly with
fork for 5 to 10 seconds. Add rehydrated vegetables to
potatoes. Make White Sauce in lid and add chicken. Serve
chicken and sauce over potatoes and vegetables.

Nutrition:
Per 2 + cups: 653 calories, 32 grams protein, 28 grams
carbohydrate, 34 grams fat

Falafel Burgers

4 burgers

Falafel burgers are great for the first or second night on trail, or when you are car-camping. Fresh tomato slices and condiments are important to balance the rather dry burgers. For cheesy burgers, place a slice of cheese on each burger after you flip it; cover the pan so the cheese will melt while the second side is browning.

1-1/2 c falafel mix
2 T oil
1 large tomato
relish, mustard, catsup, salsa, or other condiments
   to taste
4 bulky rolls

At home:
Add 2 tablespoons oil to pantry. Bag falafel mix. Pack condiments. Pack other foods.

On trail:
Rehydrate falafel mix in 1 cup cold water and let stand 20 minutes. Shape into thin burgers and brown in oil. Serve with sliced tomatoes and condiments on bulky rolls.

Nutrition:
Per burger: 376 calories, 16 grams protein, 51 grams carbohydrate, 12 grams fat

Quick Vegetable Soup

4 cups
Cook about 12 minutes

4 vegetable bouillon cubes or 8 t soup base
1 c vegetable flakes or mixed dehydrated vegetables

At home:
Bag bouillon; bag vegetables.

On trail:
Add vegetables to 4 cups water. Bring to boil and simmer 10 minutes, until vegetables are almost rehydrated. Add crushed bouillon or soup base and cook for a few more minutes.

Nutrition:
Per 1 cup: 52 calories, 3 grams protein, 9 grams carbohydrate, trace fat

Cheddar Cheese Chowder

About 5 cups
Soak 10 minutes; simmer 15 minutes

1 c dehydrated potatoes (2 medium potatoes)
1/4 t sage
1 bay leaf
1/4 t cumin
1/3 c dehydrated onion (1 medium onion)
1/2 lb grated Cheddar cheese
1-1/3 c instant powdered milk
1/4 c margarine or oil
3 T flour
1/4 t nutmeg
2 T parsley
salt and pepper to taste

At home:
Add 1/4 cup margarine or oil to pantry. Bag potatoes. Bag flour, powdered milk, nutmeg, parsley, sage, bay leaf, and cumin together. Bag cheese.

On trail:
Put potatoes in 3 cups boiling water and cook 10 minutes, or until potatoes are done. Rehydrate onion for 10 minutes in 1/3 cup hot water. Drain onions and sauté in oil. Add flour mixture to onions, stirring to make smooth. Add a little potato water to thin sauce, then add sauce to potatoes. Stir well. Add cheese to soup and cook 3 to 5 minutes, until cheese melts. Salt and pepper to taste. Quicker version: Add onions and potatoes to 3-2/3 cups boiling water and simmer about 10 minutes, until vegetables are done. Combine cheese and flour mixture, then gradually add to potatoes, stirring well. Simmer until soup thickens.

Nutrition:
Per 1-1/4 cups: 468 calories, 23 grams protein, 22 grams carbohydrate, 33 grams fat

Fish or Vegetable Chowder

3-1/2 to 4 cups
Soak 10 minutes; cook 10 to 15 minutes

1/3 c dehydrated onion (1 medium onion)
1/4 c margarine or oil
1/2 c powdered milk
1 T parsley
1 T dehydrated green pepper
1 c cooked fish
salt and pepper to taste

At home:
Add 1/4 cup margarine or oil to pantry. Bag milk and parsley together. Bag dehydrated onion and green pepper together.

On trail:
Soak onion and green pepper in 1/2 cup hot water for 10 minutes. Drain vegetables and sauté in margarine or oil. Add powdered milk mixture, stirring well. Add 2 cups water, then cooked fish. Season to taste. Serve when steaming.

You can add fresh or dehydrated corn, potatoes, peas, or other vegetables to this chowder. Corn, potatoes, and peas take 10 to 15 minutes of simmering to rehydrate, so start them early. To rehydrate, use 1 cup water for each cup of vegetables.

Nutrition:
Per 1-1/4 cups: 236 calories, 11 grams protein, 5 grams carbohydrate, 19 grams fat

Onion Soup

4 cups
Cook 5 to 10 minutes

2 T oil
1 c dehydrated onion (2 large onions)
1 T flour
4 vegetable bouillon cubes or 8 t soup base
1/8 t powdered garlic (1 clove)
1/2 c Parmesan cheese

At home:
Add 2 tablespoons oil to pantry. Bag onion separately. Bag flour, bouillon, and garlic together. Bag cheese separately.

On trail:
Rehydrate onion in 1 cup hot water for 10 minutes. Drain onion and sauté in oil. Add flour mixture and stir until smooth. Add 4 cups water, bring to boil, and simmer for 5 to 10 minutes. Serve in bowls and top with grated cheese.

Nutrition:
Per 1 cup: 155 calories, 6 grams protein, 14 grams carbohydrate, 10 grams fat

Mulligatawny Soup

4 cups
Soak 10 minutes; cook 10 to 20 minutes

1-1/2 T oil
1/2 to 1 T dehydrated green pepper
(1/4 c green pepper)
2 T dehydrated carrot (1/4 c carrot)
3 rings dehydrated apple, chopped (1/2 c apple)
1 T dehydrated onion (1/4 onion)
1 T flour
2 cubes bouillon or 4 t vegetable soup base
1 T curry powder
1/4 c shredded coconut
1/4 t powdered garlic (2 cloves)
1/2 t salt (more or less to taste)
1/2 T parsley
3 T tomato powder
1/2 c quick-cooking brown rice (optional)

At home:
Add 1-1/2 tablespoons oil to pantry. Bag vegetables and apple together. Bag flour, tomato powder, and seasonings together. Bag coconut and rice together.

On trail:
Rehydrate vegetables and apple for 10 minutes in 1/2 cup hot water (or chop fresh produce). Drain and sauté in oil. Add flour mixture, stirring well. Add 4 cups water, coconut, and rice. Cook 10 minutes, or until done. Quicker version: Skip the oil; add all ingredients to 4 cups water, bring to boil, simmer 20 minutes.

Nutrition:
Per 1-1/2 + cups: 146 calories, 2 grams protein, 19 grams carbohydrate, 8 grams fat

Potato Soup

4 cups
Total cooking time about 25 minutes

1 c dehydrated potatoes (2 medium potatoes)
3 T oil
2/3 c dehydrated onion (2 onions)
1 c instant milk powder
1/2 t salt (or more to taste) and pepper

At home:
Add 3 tablespoons oil to pantry. Bag onion and potatoes separately. Bag milk powder and salt together.

On trail:
Cook potatoes in 4 cups water until tender, about 10 minutes. Rehydrate onion for 10 minutes in 2/3 cup hot water. Sauté onion in oil; add milk powder and salt. Add 1 cup potato water to onion mixture, stirring until smooth. Add onion mixture to potatoes, stirring well. Simmer for 10 minutes. Adjust seasonings.

Nutrition:
Per 1 cup: 213 calories, 8 grams protein, 23 grams carbohydrate, 11 grams fat

Quick Barley Soup

4 cups
Cook 10 to 15 minutes

1/2 c quick-cooking barley
1/4 c dried mushrooms
scant 1/4 c dehydrated sliced carrot (1 carrot)
1/3 c dehydrated onion (1 onion)
4 cubes or 8 t vegetable bouillon
1/3 c instant milk powder

At home:
Bag dehydrated vegetables and barley. Bag bouillon and milk powder.

On trail:
Rehydrate vegetables and barley in 4 cups boiling water for 10 minutes. Add milk mixture and simmer a few more minutes, or until barley and vegetables are tender.

Nutrition:
Per 1 cup: 113 calories, 7 grams protein, 22 grams carbohydrate, 1 gram fat

Minestrone Soup

About 8 cups
Soak 10 minutes; cook about 25 minutes

1 T oil
3/4 c dehydrated cooked navy beans or
1-1/2 c freze-dried beans
1/3 c dehydrated onion (1 onion)
1/4 c dehydrated celery (5 stalks)
1/2 c dehydrated peas or 1 c freeze-dried peas
1/2 c macaroni
2 T tomato powder
2 cubes or 4 t vegetable bouillon
1 clove garlic, crushed
salt and pepper to taste

At home:
Add 1 tablespoon oil to pantry. Bag beans, celery, and peas together. Bag onion separately. Bag macaroni and seasonings together.

On trail:
Simmer bean-vegetable mixture in 5 cups hot water for 10 minutes, or until tender. Rehydrate onion separately (10 minutes in 1/3 cup hot water), drain, and sauté in oil. Add sautéed onion and macaroni mixture to beans. Cook about 15 minutes, until all ingredients are done. Quick version: Skip sautéeing onion, instead combining dehydrated onion with bean-vegetable mixture.

Nutrition:
Per 2 cups: 233 calories, 13 grams protein, 36 grams carbohydrate, 5 grams fat

Side Dishes
Mashed Potatoes

2-1/4 cups
Boil water

1-1/2 c potato flakes
1 T margarine
1/2 t salt (more or less to taste)
1-1/2 T instant powdered milk

At home:
Add 1 tablespoon margarine to pantry. Bag other ingredients together. Check recipe on package and note amount of water to add, if different from below.

On trail:
Add margarine and potato mixture to 1-1/4 cups boiling water and stir quickly with fork for 5 to 10 seconds. Let stand 1 minute before serving.

Nutrition:
Per 1 + cup: 372 calories, 21 grams protein, 59 grams carbohydrate, 7 grams fat

Carrot, Raisin, and Nut Salad

5 c shredded carrot, dehydrated (4 large carrots)
1/2 c raisins
1/2 c cashews

At home:
Bag carrots and raisins together. Bag cashews separately.

On trail:
Soak carrots and raisins in 5 cups hot water for 15 minutes, or until rehydrated. Let cool and drain liquid. Add cashews.

Nutrition:
Per 1 cup: 127 calories, 3 grams protein, 33 grams carbohydrate, 9 grams fat

Tabouli Salad

About 5 cups
Let stand 30 minutes

1 c bulgur
20 to 30 slices dehydrated tomato (2 to 3 tomatoes)
1/3 c dehydrated onion or scallions (1 onion
  or 6 scallions)
1/4 c parsley flakes
2 T mint flakes
1/4 c lemon juice
1/4 c olive oil

At home:
Bag dry ingredients. Place lemon juice and oil in one container or carry separately.

On trail:
Add 3 cups boiling water to dry ingredients, cover, and let stand 20 minutes or until bulgur is fully rehydrated. Drain excess liquid, if there is any, and then add lemon juice and oil. Let stand until cool. Season with salt and pepper.

Nutrition:
Per 1-1/2 + cups: 354 calories, 7 grams protein, 40 grams carbohydrate, 20 grams fat

Breadstuffs for Breakfast, Lunch, or Dinner

When the recipe says to bake on trail, you can choose any method you like—Dutch oven, reflector baker, Bake-Packer, Outback Oven, or an improvised method. Be sure to grease the Dutch oven and any baking pan with shortening or margarine (oil does not work as well) to prevent the baked goods from sticking.

Biscuit Mix *(make at home)*

2 cups mix

This mix can be used for pancakes, biscuits, pie dough, coffee cake, dumplings, and any other flour-based food. I prefer to use half whole wheat and half unbleached white flour, rather than all whole wheat flour, to give the biscuits a lighter texture.

1 c unbleached white flour
1 c whole wheat flour
2 t baking powder
1 t salt
2 T oil or shortening
1/3 c instant powdered milk

At home:
Combine all ingredients and put in reclosable plastic bag.

Nutrition:
Per 1 cup mix: 576 calories, 18 grams protein, 93 grams carbohydrate, 16 grams fat

Biscuits

Bake 10 minutes

On trail:
Add 1/3 cup water per 1 cup Biscuit Mix to make 6 biscuits. Bake 10 minutes, or until done.

Nutrition:
Per 6 biscuits: 576 calories, 18 grams protein, 93 grams carbohydrate, 16 grams fat

Bannock

Cook 10 minutes

Bannock is a flat pan bread, usually made with baking powder as the leavening. Make up Biscuit Mix and fry or pan-bake the dough—let dough cook on one side and then flip it over to finish cooking. Bannock is similar to pancakes, only the dough is stiffer.

Tortillas

Tortillas are easy to make and cook quickly. Use Biscuit Mix, adding 1/3 cup water to 1 cup mix. Knead the dough until it is smooth. Pinch off a ball of dough and flatten until it is paper-thin. Use as little oil in the pan as possible—tortillas should pan-bake rather than fry. One cup Biscuit Mix makes 6 tortillas.

Cornbread

9 pieces
Bake 20 minutes

2 T oil
1 c flour, whole wheat and/or unbleached white
3/4 c cornmeal
1/3 c sugar
1/3 c instant powdered milk
3/4 t salt
2 T egg powder
3 t baking powder

At home:

Add 2 tablespoons oil to pantry. Combine remaining ingredients and bag together. Makes about 2 cups dry mix.

On trail:

Add oil and 1 cup plus 2 tablespoons water to dry ingredients and mix. Bake in 8-by-8-inch pan for 20 minutes in a reflector baker or other baker.

Nutrition:

Per piece: 211 calories, 8 grams protein, 58 grams carbohydrate, 11 grams fat

Coffee Cake

6 pieces
Bake 25 minutes

2 c Biscuit Mix
1/2 c brown sugar
1/3 c oatmeal
1/4 c margarine
1 t cinnamon

At home:
Add 1/4 cup margarine to pantry. Bag Biscuit Mix and 2 tablespoons sugar together. Bag remaining sugar, oatmeal, and cinnamon together.

On trail:
Add 2/3 cup water (or more as necessary) to biscuit mixture and spoon into greased pan. Add 1/4 cup margarine to oatmeal mixture to make topping and sprinkle over batter. Bake for 25 minutes, or until done.

Nutrition:
Per piece: 334 calories, 8 grams protein, 50 grams carbohydrate, 10 grams fat

Donuts

About 12 small donuts

I made donuts on a layover day on the Dubawnt River trip (see Chapter 11). We had extra shortening and we needed the calories. The finger-sized crullers were a true trail delicacy.

1/3 c water
1 c Biscuit Mix
2 T honey
1 t cinnamon
fat for frying (about 1 c per 1 c Biscuit Mix)

On trail:
Combine Biscuit Mix, water, honey, and cinnamon. Stir well and knead dough until smooth. Pat into 1/2-inch-thick slab. Cut into pieces about 4 inches long and 1/2-inch wide. Fry in hot fat, removing when golden brown. If the fat is too cool, the donuts will be greasy; if it is too hot, the donuts will burn. When the dough hits the grease, sinks to the bottom, and then bounces back to the surface, bubbling all the while, you'll get crispy, tender donuts.

Nutrition:
Per 4 donuts: 432 calories, 6 grams protein, 42 grams carbohydrate, 28 grams fat

Notes on Using a BakePacker

If you are using a BakePacker, use the following guidelines for amounts and baking times, as per the instructions that come with the device. If you add raisins, fruit, or nuts, add 3 to 5 minutes to baking time. The consistency of batter should be neither runny nor stiff; it should be halfway between the consistency of pancakes and that of bread dough. Because food baked in a plastic bag does not lose any moisture, it is important that the dough be the right consistency. Mixes that are formulated for the BakePacker call for slightly less liquid than do recipes designed for a conventional oven.

For the Standard (7-3/8-inch) BakePacker

Serves 1–2: 3/4 cup dry mix; bake 8 to 10 minutes, let stand 3 minutes

Serves 2–3: 1-1/2 cups dry mix; bake 15 to 18 minutes, let stand 5 minutes

Serves 4–6: 3 cups dry mix; bake 22 to 26 minutes, let stand 5 minutes

For the Ultra-Light (5-3/4-inch) BakePacker

Serves 1–2: 3/4 cup dry mix; bake 8 to 10 minutes, let stand 3 minutes

Serves 2–3: 1-1/2 cups dry mix; bake 15 to 18 minutes, let stand 5 minutes

Sauces

A good sauce can transform bland noodles into a gourmet meal. Unless otherwise indicated, allow about 1/2 cup sauce for 1 cup cooked pasta or grain.

Tomato Sauce

2 cups
Cook about 15 minutes

You can make a very simple sauce with tomato powder and herbs, but the sauce becomes richer with the addition of vegetables. You don't have to stick with the vegetables listed. If you have a dehydrator, you can experiment with broccoli, spinach, or anything else that sounds good. Serve this sauce over lentils, pasta, or any grain.

2/3 c tomato powder
2 t mixed herbs (basil, oregano, thyme, garlic)
salt (to taste)
16 to 20 slices dehydrated tomato
3 T dehydrated onion (1/2 onion)
2 T dehydrated green pepper
1/4 c dehydrated mushrooms

At home:
Combine tomato powder and herbs in one bag and the dehydrated vegetables in another.

On trail:
Add vegetables to 2 cups water, bring to boil, and simmer about 10 minutes. Add tomato powder and herbs. Simmer until the flavor has developed or until you are ready to eat, whichever comes first. Tomato sauce is good when topped with fresh Parmesan cheese.

Nutrition:
Per 1/2 cup: 88 calories, 4 grams protein, 20 grams carbohydrate, trace fat

White Sauce

1 cup
Cook 5 to 8 minutes

White Sauce is boring by itself unless you spice it up, but it is the base for several other sauces.

2 T margarine
2 T flour
1/3 c instant powdered milk
1 c water
salt and pepper to taste
seasonings (below, optional)

At home:
Add 2 tablespoons margarine to pantry. Bag flour and milk together.

On trail:
Melt margarine over low flame. Continue to cook, stirring in flour mixture to form a smooth paste. Slowly add 1 cup water, stirring briskly. Add seasonings and cook several minutes until thick.

To pep up the sauce, you can add one or more of the following ingredients:

1/2 t Worcestershire sauce
2 T parsely
2 T chopped chives
1 T dried onion, rehydrated and sautéed

Nutrition:
Per 1/2 cup: 168 calories, 5 grams protein, 17 grams carbohydrate, 12 grams fat

Cheese Sauce

About 2 cups
Cook 8 to 10 minutes

Serve Cheese Sauce over lentils, pasta, or any grain.

1 c White Sauce (page 99)
1 c grated Cheddar cheese

At home:
Prepare White Sauce ingredients. Bag cheese and seasonings together.

On trail:
Make White Sauce and add grated cheese and seasonings. Stir until the cheese has melted.

To spice up this sauce, you can add to the cheese one of the following:

1/8 t paprika
dash of cayenne
1/2 t dry mustard

Nutrition:
Per 1/2 cup: 340 calories, 16 grams protein, 18 grams carbohydrate, 26 grams fat

Florentine Sauce

About 2 cups
Let stand 10 minutes; cook 8 minutes

1 c White Sauce (page 99)
4 drops Worcestershire sauce
1/2 c dehydrated spinach (1 cup fresh)
1 T parsley
pinch of nutmeg
salt and pepper to taste

At home:
Prepare White Sauce ingredients, adding Worcestershire sauce and nutmeg to flour mixture. Bag fresh or dehydrated spinach.

On trail:
Rehydrate spinach in 1/2 cup hot water for 10 or more minutes. Prepare White Sauce. Add spinach, salt, and pepper. Cook until spinach is tender.

Nutrition:
Per 1 cup: 195 calories, 8 grams protein, 22 grams carbohydrate, 12 grams fat

Bouillon Sauce

1 cup
Cook 5 to 8 minutes

2 T margarine
2 T flour
1 cube bouillon or 2 t soup base
2 drops Worcestershire sauce (optional)
salt and pepper to taste

At home:
Add 2 tablespoons margarine to pantry. Bag other ingredients together; if using bouillon, crush cube.

On trail:
Melt margarine and add flour mixture, stirring to form smooth paste. Add 1 cup water. Stir well and cook until sauce thickens.

Nutrition:
Per 1/2 cup: 129 calories, 2 grams protein, 6 grams carbohydrate, 12 grams fat

Bouillon Sauce with Vegetables

At home:
Bag 1/2 cup dried vegetables together, using a mixture of tomatoes, green peppers, onions or scallions, and mushrooms. Add an extra bouillon cube or 2 teaspoons extra powder to the sauce bag.

On trail:
Simmer vegetables in 1/2 cup (more if needed) hot water for 10 minutes. Make sauce. Add vegetables after sauce has thickened.

Bouillon Sauce with Mushrooms

Follow directions for Bouillon Sauce with Vegetables, but use 1/2 cup mushrooms.

Peanut Sauce or Gado-Gado

About 1-1/4 cups
Cook about 5 minutes

This sauce has a hearty flavor but, surprisingly, does not taste like peanut butter. If you're tired of cheese and tomato sauces, give it a try. Serve over spaghetti.

2 cubes bouillon or 4 t soup base
1/4 c peanut butter
1 t tamari or soy sauce
2 T instant powdered milk
dash garlic

At home:
Bag all ingredients together.

On trail:
Put all ingredients in a small pot and add 1 cup water. Stir briskly over low heat for about 5 minutes, until sauce thickens.

Nutrition:
Per 1/2 + cup: 211 calories, 11 grams protein, 9 grams carbohydrate, 16 grams fat

Quick Curry Sauce

1 cup
Let stand 10 minutes; cook 8 to 10 minutes

Serve over rice.

1/3 c dehydrated onion (1 onion)
3 T margarine
3 T flour
1 cube bouillon or 2 t soup base (chicken
or vegetable)
1 t curry powder
dash garlic powder
salt (to taste)

At home:
Add 3 tablespoons margarine to pantry. Bag onion. Bag flour and seasonings.

On trail:
Rehydrate onion in 1/3 cup hot water for 10 minutes. Drain. Sauté onion in margarine, then add flour and seasonings. Add 1 cup water, stirring briskly. Bring sauce to a boil and then simmer for several minutes.

Nutrition:
Per 1/2 cup: 219 calories, 3 grams protein, 15 grams carbohydrate, 18 grams fat

Lemon Sauce

1/2 cup
Cook 2 to 3 minutes

If you are planning on fishing, take some extra margarine and lemon juice in your pantry to make this simple sauce, which is wonderful on freshly fried fish.

1/3 c margarine
dash garlic powder
3 T lemon juice
salt and pepper to taste

On trail:
Combine ingredients in small pan and simmer until they are well blended. Serve over fish.

Nutrition:
Per 2 tablespoons: 136 calories, no protein, 1 gram carbohydrate, 16 grams fat

Chili Sauce

About 2 cups
Soak 10 minutes; cook 5 minutes

This sauce is excellent served over lentils or bulgur.

1 T oil or margarine
1 T flour
1 clove fresh garlic or 1/2 t powdered
1-1/2 t (or more to taste) chili powder
1/4 t dry mustard
1/4 t ground cumin
1/8 t celery seeds (optional)
1/8 t black pepper
2 T tomato powder
1/4 c dehydrated onion (1/2 large onion, diced)
1/4 c dehydrated green pepper
**   (1 large green pepper)**
15 slices dehydrated tomato (3 medium tomatoes)

At home:
Add 1 tablespoon oil to pantry. Combine seasonings in film container. Bag dehydrated vegetables. Bag flour.

On trail:
Rehydrate vegetables in 1 cup hot water, or more if necessary, for 10 minutes. In another pot, sauté seasonings in oil; add flour. Add rehydrated vegetables and water. Bring to a boil and simmer 5 minutes.

Nutrition:
Per 1/2 cup: 58 calories, 1 gram protein, 5 grams carbohydrate, 4 grams fat

Pesto *(make at home)*

About 1-1/2 cup

Pesto on spaghetti is one of my favorite dishes for the first or second night out. It is simple, elegant, and filling. Pesto made from dry packaged mixes simply does not compare with fresh or frozen. If you do not have access to fresh basil to make your own pesto, check your supermarket's specialty section. Many markets now carry prepared pesto.

This is the recipe I use, but I adjust the amounts to taste, and so should you. Although the traditional recipe calls for pine nuts, they are both expensive and hard to find in rural Maine. I use walnuts—a heresy, I'm sure—but no one has ever complained. If you are truly decadent, as I am, sprinkle on a bit more Parmesan cheese as you serve the pesto.

4 c packed fresh basil leaves
1/2 c olive oil
2 cloves garlic
6 sprigs parsley
1/4 c pine nuts or walnuts
1/2 c grated Parmesan cheese
salt and pepper to taste

At home:
Put all ingredients in a food processor and blend for 10 seconds or until ingredients are well chopped and mixed. Put into a plastic container or reclosable bag. Store in the refrigerator if you are going to use it within a few days, otherwise store in the freezer. Double-bag for the trail.

On trail:
Mix with cooked spaghetti.

Nutrition:
Per 1/4 cup: 144 calories, 6 grams protein, 2 grams carbohydrate, 21 grams fat

Salsa

Salsa will keep unrefrigerated for several days, so if you have a favorite brand, take it along in a plastic container with an extra plastic bag for safety. You can also dehydrate salsa by spreading it on a nonstick or slightly oiled tray and drying it in an oven or dehydrator at 130 degrees (see Chapter 3). The salsa "leather" should be just that— leathery. Store in an airtight container and rehydrate in hot water as you need it on trail.

You can make a quick trail salsa of equal parts dehydrated tomatoes, green peppers, and onion, plus chili pepper to taste. Soak these dried vegetables in hot water for 10 minutes for a crunchy but edible salsa, or simmer them 10 minutes for a more fully rehydrated sauce.

Desserts

I tried to devise a recipe for no-cook, no-bake cookies. The resulting "cookies" tasted, not surprisingly, like raw dough. I then tried to come up with a recipe that involved cooking but not baking the dough. These "cookies" were overwhelmingly sweet and not very good. The moral of the story is that if you really want to have cookies on trail, take some from home. There are other desserts, including delicious cakes, that require less time and less fuel—and you get more dessert for your efforts.

When a recipe calls for dried fruit, you can use apples, pears, peaches, some other fruit, or a combination of several fruits. (Some stores sell a mixture of chopped dried fruit.) Nutritional calculations here are based on mixed fruit; values will vary slightly depending on what you choose.

Stewed Fruit

2 cups
Cook 5 to 10 minutes

If you want more calories, add a spoonful of margarine.

1 c dried apples or mixed dried fruit
1/2 t cinnamon
2 t honey or brown sugar (optional)

At home:
Chop fruit and bag with other ingredients.

On trail:
Add ingredients to 2 cups water and cook 5 to 10 minutes over low heat until fruit is tender.

Nutrition:
Per 1 cup stewed apples: 63 calories, trace protein, 16 grams carbohydrate, trace fat; per 1 cup stewed mixed fruit: 131 calories, 2 grams protein, 83 grams carbohydrate, 2 grams fat

Rice Pudding

2 cups
Cook 5 to 10 minutes

If you are planning a rice dinner, cook 2 cups extra and use it in rice pudding. Or you can use instant rice.

1 c instant rice, uncooked
1/2 c raisins
1 t cinnamon
1/4 c instant milk powder
1/4 to 1/2 c honey or brown sugar
1 t lemon rind or 1/2 t lemon flavoring (optional)

At home:
Combine ingredients and bag.

On trail:
Add mixture to 2 cups boiling water. Simmer for 5 minutes, or until rice is done.

Nutrition:
Per 1/2 cup serving (using 1/2 cup honey): 309 calories, 8 grams protein, 76 grams carbohydrate, 1 gram fat

Spiced Fruit Rice Pudding

About 4-1/2 cups
Cook 5 to 10 minutes

This dessert, which can also be served as breakfast, offers a nice change from the traditional rice pudding. Again, you can substitute cooked rice if you have some left over from the previous meal.

3/4 c instant brown rice, uncooked
1/2 c instant milk powder
1/2 t nutmeg
2 T lemon juice or 1/2 t lemon flavoring
1/4 c honey
1/2 t cinnamon
1/4 t ginger
1-1/2 c dried fruit

At home:
Chop dried fruit and bag together with other ingredients.

On trail:
Add ingredients to 2-1/2 cups water. Bring to boil and simmer until rice is cooked and dried fruit is tender, 5 to 10 minutes. Stir well so pudding does not burn.

Nutrition:
Per 1/2 + cup: 194 calories, 3 grams protein, 48 grams carbohydrate, 1 gram fat; per 1 + cup: 388 calories, 6 grams protein, 96 grams carbohydrate, 2 grams fat

Danish Dried Fruit Soup

5 cups
Cook 10 minutes

1/4 c each dried apples, apricots, pears, pitted
  prunes, peaches, and raisins, or 1-1/2 c mixed
  dried fruit
1 to 2 whole cloves
3 T quick-cooking tapioca
1/3 c brown sugar
1 t cinnamon
1 T lemon rind or 1/2 t lemon flavoring

At home:
Dice fruit. Bag all ingredients together.

On trail:
Add mixture to 5 cups water and bring to boil, simmering
about 10 minutes, until fruit is tender.

Nutrition:
Per 1-1/4 cup: 317 calories, 2 grams protein, 82 grams
carbohydrate, 2 grams fat

Berry Pie

1 9-inch pie
Bake 40 minutes

If you do not have a 9-inch pot lid with a raised lip, use two smaller pot lids that together would hold that amount.

1 c Biscuit Mix
1/4 c shortening
3 to 4 c berries
1/2 c sugar or honey
3 T cornstarch or flour
1 t cinnamon
1 T margarine (optional)

At home:
Cut shortening into Biscuit Mix and bag; this is the crust mix. Bag sugar, cornstarch or flour, and cinnamon together. Add 1·tablespoon margarine to pantry.

On trail:
Pick berries. Add 2 tablespoons water to crust mix and mix well; you may need to add more water. Pat dough into one or two pans, bringing up the edges of the dough. Make filling by combining berries and remaining ingredients. Bake hot (equivalent to 425 degrees) for 40 minutes.

Nutrition:
Per quarter-pie: 458 calories, 8 grams protein, 75 grams carbohydrate, 18 grams fat

Tapioca Pudding

3 cups
Cook about 5 minutes; let stand for 20 minutes

Experiment with different flavorings, such as cherry, maple walnut, orange, or maple.

1/3 c sugar
3 T quick-cooking tapioca
1 c instant milk powder
2 T powdered egg (optional)
1 t vanilla or other flavoring

At home:
Bag all ingredients except flavoring. Place flavoring in film canister.

On trail:
Add tapioca mixture to 2-3/4 cups water, stirring to dissolve eggs and milk. Let stand 5 minutes. Place over heat and stir until mixture comes to a full boil. Remove from heat, stir in vanilla or other flavoring, and let cool 20 minutes.

Nutrition:
Per 3/4-cup (without egg): 150 calories, 8 grams protein, 31 grams carbohydrate, trace fat

Fruit Crunch

6-inch round
Cook 10 minutes; bake 20 minutes

You can make this recipe using any dried fruit. Pear Crunch and Cherry Crunch are particularly good.

1/3 c brown sugar
1/2 c flour
1/2 c oatmeal
1/8 t baking powder
1/8 t baking soda
1/8 t salt
1/4 c margarine
2 t quick-cooking tapioca
1/2 c dry fruit

At home:
Add 1/4 cup margarine to pantry. Bag tapioca and fruit together. Bag remaining ingredients together, which will be the crust.

On trail:
Add tapioca and fruit to 1/2 cup hot water and cook for 10 minutes, adding more water if necessary. Add margarine to crust ingredients and mix well. Put half of the crust mixture in a 6-inch pan, pressing down to make a flat layer. Spoon the fruit mixture onto the bottom crust and then cover the fruit with the remaining crust. Bake 20 minutes, or bake 15 minutes and let stand 5 minutes. (Fits in Ultra-Light BakePacker.)

Nutrition:
Per quarter-recipe: 339 calories, 4 grams protein, 57 grams carbohydrate, 13 grams fat

Fruit Cobbler

4 + cups
Cook a total of 10 minutes; let stand 5 minutes

2 c dried fruit
1/3 c brown sugar
1/2 t cinnamon
pinch nutmeg
pinch cloves
1 t lemon rind or 1/2 t lemon flavoring
1/2 c Biscuit Mix

At home:
Bag 2 tablespoons brown sugar together with Biscuit Mix; bag remaining ingredients together.

On trail:
Put fruit mixture into pot with 3 cups water and bring to boil; simmer 5 minutes. Add 2 tablespoons water to Biscuit Mix and mix well. Spread Biscuit Mix evenly over apples. Cover and cook for 5 minutes. Let stand 5 minutes.

Nutrition:
Per 1 + cup: 416 calories, 4 grams protein, 104 grams carbohydrate, 3 grams fat

Ginger Crisp

About 5 cups
Bake 15 minutes; let stand 5 minutes

1-1/2 c dried fruit
1 c crushed gingersnap cookies
1/3 c brown sugar
3 T margarine
1/4 t salt

At home:

Add 1/4 cup margarine to pantry. Bag fruit separately. Bag cookies, sugar, and salt together.

On trail:

Put fruit into a pot with 2-1/2 cups water and bring to boil; simmer 5 minutes or until most of the water has been absorbed; drain. Add margarine to cookies and mix well; spread over rehydrated fruit. Bake 10 minutes and let stand 5 minutes. (Fits in Standard BakePacker.)

Nutrition:

Per 1 cup: 397 calories, 2 grams protein, 106 grams carbohydrate, 11 grams fat

Golden Cake

One layer, 7- or 8-inch diameter
Bake 20 minutes; let stand 5 minutes

3/4 c flour
1-1/2 T instant milk powder
1-1/2 t baking powder
1/8 t salt
4 T powdered eggs
2 T margarine
1/3 c sugar

At home:
Add 2 tablespoons margarine to pantry. Combine other ingredients and bag.

On trail:
Add margarine to dry ingredients and mix well, then add 1/3 cup plus 1 tablespoon water and mix well. Bake 20 minutes and let stand 5 minutes. (Fits in Standard BakePacker.)

Nutrition:
Per quarter-cake: 230 calories, 5 grams protein, 132 grams carbohydrate, 8 grams fat

Golden Cake Variations

For Chocolate Cake: Add 1/4 cup cocoa powder and increase sugar to 1/2 cup.

For Spice Cake: Add 1/2 teaspoon cinnamon, 1/2 teaspoon cloves, and 1/4 teaspoon allspice to dry mix. Decrease sugar by 1 tablespoon and add 1 tablespoon molasses.

For Gingerbread: Add 1/2 teaspoon ginger to dry mix. Decrease sugar to 2 tablespoons and add 1/4 cup molasses.

For Upside-Down Cake: Simmer 8 to 10 dried apricot halves or 4 dehydrated pineapple rings in 1 cup water until tender. Drain. Melt 1/4 cup margarine in baking pan. Add 2/3 cup brown sugar and spread evenly in pan. Place fruit over brown sugar mixture and cover with Golden Cake batter. Bake for 25 minutes.

For BakePacker Apricot Right-Side-Up Cake: Simmer 8 to 10 dried apricot halves in 1 cup water until fruit is tender. Drain. Make Golden Cake in plastic bag and spread bag on BakePacker grid. Lay apricots on top of batter; sprinkle 1/4 cup brown sugar over apricots. Bake 25 minutes and let stand 5 minutes.

Chocolate Buttermilk Cake

One layer, 7- or 8-inch diameter
Bake 20 minutes; let stand 5 minutes

This cake is delicious, but because it does not have eggs it crumbles easily and should be eaten as soon as it is done. Keep your bowl and spoon handy. You can add 2 to 4 tablespoons powdered eggs to prevent crumbling.

3/4 c flour
1/2 c sugar
1/4 c cocoa powder
1/2 t baking soda
1/4 t salt
2 T buttermilk powder
1/4 c oil (not olive)

At home:
Add 1/4 cup oil to pantry. Bag remaining ingredients together.

On trail:
Add 1/2 cup water and oil to dry ingredients and mix well. Bake 20 minutes, then let stand 5 minutes. (Fits in Standard BakePacker.)

Nutrition:
Per quarter-cake: 324 calories, 4 grams protein, 46 grams carbohydrate, 15 grams fat

Fruitcake *(make at home)*

1 loaf, 10 slices
Bake 1-1/4 hours; let stand 30 minutes

The birthday of one of my students fell during a winter camping trip. The three pounds of fruitcake that weighed down my pack were just what we needed when the thermometer dropped to –34 degrees Fahrenheit. Use this recipe if you do not have a family favorite.

1/2 lb diced dried fruit (peaches, pears, prunes, apricots)
1 c raisins
1 c currants
1/2 c flour
1/4 t baking soda
1/2 t cinnamon
1/4 t allspice
1/4 t mace
1/4 t ground cloves
1/4 c oil or softened shortening
1/3 c brown sugar
1/4 t lemon flavoring
1 egg
1/4 c molasses
1/4 c milk
3 c chopped pecans or walnuts

At home:
Cover dried fruit with boiling water and let stand 2 hours. Sift together flour, soda, and spices. In separate bowl, beat together shortening, sugar, and extract; add egg, molasses, milk, and nuts. Drain excess water from fruit, and add fruit to batter. Stir well. Spoon into loaf pan lined with aluminum foil. Bake at 325 degrees for about 1-1/4 hours. Remove from oven and cool in pan for 30 minutes. When loaf is cool and firm, slice into desired portions, wrap

carefully, and store in cool place. Preslicing the cake simplifies serving it on trail, especially if you take it on a winter trip.

Nutrition:
Per 1 slice (using walnuts): 513 calories, 11 grams protein, 61 grams carbohydrate, 29 grams fat

Hot Drinks

There are dozens of wonderful teas on the market, from black teas to herbal varieties. Choose a tea or teas that you know you like; take several different kinds so you will have a choice. Tea bags are light, so don't economize. I have not included directions for making coffee because every coffee drinker I know has his or her own preferred way of making it on trail.

I have designated sugar in some hot drinks because it is easy to buy and pack. The hot milk drinks are good with honey (or powdered honey) instead of sugar. If you substitute honey, cut back the sweetening by about one-third.

Soup can be considered a "cup of something hot" before dinner. The instant soups listed here, in one-person and six-person amounts, can help you stay hydrated and give you a tasty hot drink to keep you going until dinner. These recipes call for boiling water but do not require cooking. If you are traveling in cold weather and you have room for a thermos, carry hot water and an instant soup for lunch.

In winter, when you need lots of calories, drink hot beverages, such as cocoa and soup, that have calories—coffee and tea do not.

Hot Chocolate

You don't have to buy the commercial mixes that have additives in them. It is very easy to make your own hot chocolate mix at home. Some people like more sugar than what I've given here; I like mine on the less-sweet side.

	for 1 cup	*for 4 cups*
Cocoa	1-1/2 T	1/3 c
Sugar	1/2 to 1 T	2 to 4 T
Salt	dash	1/8 t
Instant powdered milk	1/3 c	1-1/3 c

At home:
Combine and bag ingredients.

On trail:
Mix ingredients. Use 1/2 cup plus 1 tablespoon mix with 1 cup boiling water.

Nutrition:
Per 1 cup (using 1 tablespoon sugar): 149 calories, 10 grams protein, 26 grams carbohydrate, 2 grams fat

Hot Chocolate Variations

For Carob Hot Milk: Substitute carob for cocoa.

For Trail Mexican Hot Chocolate, add:

Cinnamon   1/8 t (for 1 cup); 1/2 t (for 4 cups)
Ground almonds   1 T (for 1 cup); 1/4 c (for 4 cups)

Use 1/2 cup plus 2 tablespoons mix per serving with 1 cup boiling water.

For Mocha Hot Chocolate, add:

Instant coffee   1 T (for 1 cup); 4 T (for 4 cups)

Use 1/2 cup plus 2 tablespoons mix per serving with 1 cup boiling water.

For Spiced Hot Milk, leave out the cocoa and add:

Cinnamon   1/8 t (for 1 cup); 1/2 t (for 4 cups)

Use 6-1/2 tablespoons (slightly more than 1/3 cup) mix per serving with 1 cup boiling water.

Bouillon

1 cup

This is the easiest recipe in the book. I include it because people often forget about bouillon when they head for the trail.

1 cube bouillon or 2 t soup base

At home:
Bag bouillon.

On trail:
Add 1 cup boiling water to crushed bouillon cube or soup base. Stir to dissolve.

Nutrition:
Per 1 cup: 5 calories, 1 gram protein, trace carbohydrate and fat

Milford Cushman

Instant Tomato–
Black Bean Soup

Let stand 5 minutes

	for 1 cup	*for 6 cups*
Tomato powder	2 t	1/4 c
Black bean powder	2 t	1/4 c
Salt	generous dash	1/4 t
Garlic powder	generous dash	1/8 t
Chili powder	generous dash	1/8 t or more to taste

At home:
Combine ingredients and bag.

On trail:
Put 2 tablespoons soup mix in insulated mug and add 1 cup boiling water. Cover and let stand 5 minutes.

Nutrition:
Per 1 cup: 32 calories, 2 grams protein, 6 grams carbohydrate, trace fat

Instant Tomato Soup

Let stand 5 minutes

	for 1 cup	*for 6 cups*
Tomato powder	2 t	1/4 c
Potato flakes	4 t	1/2 c
Mixture of basil, oregano, and thyme	1 t	2 T
Salt	generous dash	1/4 t
Garlic	generous dash	1/8 t
Parmesan cheese (optional)	1 T	1/4 c plus 2 T

At home:
Combine ingredients and bag.

On trail:
Put 2 tablespoons soup mix (3 tablespoons if you use cheese) in insulated mug and add 1 cup boiling water. Cover and let stand 5 minutes.

Nutrition:
Per 1 cup (with cheese): 43 calories, 3 grams protein, 5 grams carbohydrate, 4 grams fat

Instant Trail Minestrone Soup

Let stand 10 minutes

	for 1 cup	for 6 cups
Pasta	1 T	1/4 c plus 2 T
Mixed vegetables	1/4 c	1-1/2 c
Mixture of oregano, basil, and thyme	1/2 t	1 T
Bouillon or beef-flavored soup base	1 cube or 2 t	6 cubes or 4 T

At the store:
Buy a type of pasta, like angel hair pasta, that cooks in 5 minutes or less.

At home:
Choose dried vegetables such as grated carrots and thin slices of mushrooms, green pepper, tomato, and scallions, which rehydrate quickly. You can also include onion, though with only 10 minutes to rehydrate, it will still be tough. Crush the bouillon cube. Bag all ingredients together.

On trail:
Thoroughly mix ingredients. Put 1/4 cup plus 1-1/2 tablespoons mix in insulated mug and add 1 cup boiling water. Cover and let stand 10 minutes.

Nutrition:
Per 1 cup: 80 calories, 4 grams protein, 12 grams carbohydrate, trace fat

Instant Almond Soup

Let stand 3 minutes

	for 1 cup	*for 6 cups*
Bouillon or soup base	1 cube or 2 t	6 cubes or 4 T
Ground almonds	1 T	1/4 c plus 2 T
Instant powdered milk	1 T	1/4 c plus 2 T
Salt and pepper to taste		

At home:
Bag all ingredients.

On trail:
Add 1/4 cup plus scant 1 tablespoon mix into insulated mug and add 1 cup boiling water. Cover and let stand 3 minutes.

Nutrition:
Per 1 cup: 74 calories, 5 grams protein, 4 grams carbohydrate, 5 grams fat

Mexican Oatmeal Soup

Let stand 10 minutes

This is a strange-sounding recipe, but the soup is actually quite good. No one has ever guessed that it has oatmeal in it.

	for 1 cup	*for 6 cups*
Rolled oats, quick-cooking	1/4 c	1-1/2 c
Dehydrated onion	3 T	1/2 c
Powdered garlic	generous dash	3/4 t
Salt	generous dash	3/4 t
Bouillon or soup base	1/2 cube or 1 t	3 cubes or 3 T
Tomato powder	1 T	1/4 plus 2 T

At home:
Place oats in a skillet and brown over medium heat. Bag all ingredients together when oats have cooled.

On trail:
Mix ingredients well. Put 1/2 cup soup mix in insulated mug and add 1 cup boiling water. Let stand 10 minutes.

Nutrition:
Per 1 cup: 113 calories, 6 grams protein, 24 grams carbohydrate, 2 grams fat

Instant Cashew and Carrot Soup

Let stand 10 minutes

	for 1 cup	for 6 cups
Dehydrated onion	1 T	1/4 c plus 2 T
Dehydrated carrot (shredded)	1 T	1/4 c plus 2 T
Dehydrated apple	2 T	3/4 c
Instant rice	1 T	1/4 c plus 2 T
Tomato powder	2 t	1/4 c
Raisins	1 T	1/4 c plus 2 T
Cashews, chopped	1 T	1/4 c plus 2 T
Curry	generous dash	1/2 t
Salt	1/8 t	3/4 t
Garlic powder	dash	1/4 t

At home:
Combine ingredients and bag.

On trail:
Put 1/2 cup soup mix in insulated mug and add 1 cup boiling water. Let stand for 10 minutes.

Nutrition:
Per 1 cup: 131 calories, 3 grams protein, 23 grams carbohydrate, 4 grams fat

7
Food Values

Values given in the following table are from *Nutritive Value of American Foods in Common Units, Nutritive Value of Foods,* package labels, and other sources. In some cases, the value is an average of several brands and in others the value is for one representative brand. Since values vary by brand and by recipe, the granola bar you buy may have slightly different nutritional numbers than the ones listed here.

This list does not include every food that might be taken on camping trips, nor have these products been screened for additives.

Because of the process by which food values are derived, there are inconsistencies between the caloric value listed in the table and the caloric value derived from the grams of protein, carbohydrate, and fat. In other words, if you multiply the grams of protein and carbohydrate by 4 and the grams of fat by 9 and then add those two figures, the result may not equal the total presented in the calories column. Use column 2 for caloric values and columns 3, 4, and 5 to obtain information about the balance of calories from protein, carbohydrate, and fat.

Fractions have been rounded to the nearest whole number.

"Tr" means that the nutrient is present in trace quantities.

134

If a food is listed in cooked form, then the weight listed will be for the cooked product.

In some cases, values were not available.

When whole and dehydrated foods are listed together in one entry, the weight has not been included.

Nutritive Values

	Weight (grams)	Calories	Protein (grams)	Carbohydrate (grams)	Fat (grams)
Almond butter, 1 T	16	101	2	3	10
Almonds, 1 c (about 5 oz)	142	850	26	28	77
Almonds, scant 1/4 c (1 oz)	28	167	6	6	15
Apples, raw, 1 (about 3/4 c dehydrated)	—	70	Tr	18	Tr
Apples, dried, 1 c	—	91	Tr	23	Tr
Apples, dried, 10 rings	64	155	1	42	Tr
Apricots, raw, 1	38	18	1	5	0
Apricots, dried, 10 halves (2 oz)	57	140	2	35	Tr
Bacon, 2 slices, fried	15	90	5	1	8
Bagels, 1	84	280	8	53	3
Bananas, raw, 1 medium	175	100	1	26	Tr
Banana flakes, 1 c	100	340	4	89	1
Barley, quick-cooking, 1/2 c uncooked	72	255	8	54	2
Beans, baked, 1 c cooked	224	290	15	42	7
Beans, black, powdered, 1 c	100	340	20	58	3
Beans, garbanzo, 1 c cooked	227	210	12	36	4
Beans, green, cooked, 1 c	125	30	2	7	Tr
Beans, kidney, 1/2 c dry (6.4 oz)	182	280	19	66	2
Beans, navy, 1/2 c dry (6.4 oz)	182	275	19	46	2
Beans, refried, 1 c cooked	225	228	14	38	2
Beans, refried, powdered, 1 c	100	340	20	58	2
Beef, top round, 3.5 oz, into jerky	—	211	31	0	9
Beef, 1 pound into jerky	—	970	143	0	41
Biscuit mix, unbleached flour, 1/2 c (2 oz)	57	240	4	37	8
Biscuit mix, 1 c (4 oz)	114	480	8	74	16
Biscuits, 1	28	90	2	15	3
Blackberries, raw, 1 c	144	85	2	19	1
Blueberries, raw, 1 c	140	85	1	21	1
Bouillon cubes, 1	4	5	1	Tr	Tr
Bread, whole wheat, 1 slice	28	65	3	14	1

(Continued on next page)

Nutritive Values *(continued)*

	Weight (grams)	Calories	Protein (grams)	Carbohydrate (grams)	Fat (grams)
Brownies, 1	20	85	1	13	4
Bulgur, 1/2 c uncooked	—	227	8	47	1
Butter-flavored granules, 1 t dry	2	8	0	2	Tr
Cake, devil's food, 1 piece	69	235	3	40	9
Candy, hard, 1 oz	28	110	0	28	Tr
Carrots, 1 small (scant 1/3 c dehydrated)	—	20	1	5	Tr
Celery, 1/2 c chopped (3/4 to 1 T dehydrated)	—	11	Tr	3	Tr
Cashew butter, 1 oz	28	167	5	8	14
Cashew nuts, raw, scant 1/4 c (1 oz)	28	157	5	8	13
Cashew nuts, roasted, 1 c (about 5 oz)	140	785	24	41	64
Cheese, Cheddar, 1 cu in	17	70	4	Tr	6
Cheese, Cheddar, 1 oz (1/3 c grated)	28	115	7	1	9
Cheese, mozzarella, low moisture/part skim, 1 oz	28	80	8	0	5
Cheese, Parmesan, 1 oz (1/3 c grated)	28	110	11	1	7
Chicken, canned, boneless, 3 oz	85	170	18	0	10
Chicken noodle soup, dehydrated, 2 oz package	57	220	8	33	6
Chocolate, milk, plain, 1 oz	28	145	2	16	9
Chocolate bits, 1 c	170	860	7	97	61
Cocoa, hot, 1 pkt mix, 1 oz	28	110	1	24	1
Coconut, dried, sweetened, shredded, 1 c	93	466	3	44	33
Cookies, chocolate chip, 1	10	50	1	7	2
Cookies, fig bars, 1	14	50	1	11	1
Corn, 1/2 c raw (1/4 c dehydrated)	—	67	3	17	Tr
Corn grits, instant, white, 1 pkt (makes 4/5 c cooked)	23	79	2	18	Tr
Cornmeal, degermed, cooked, 1 c	138	500	11	108	2
Cornbread, 1/6 of 8-inch round, from mix	—	180	3	27	7

(Continued on next page)

Nutritive Values *(continued)*

	Weight (grams)	Calories	Protein (grams)	Carbohydrate (grams)	Fat (grams)
Cornbread mix, dry, for					
8-inch round	198	1080	18	162	42
Couscous, 1/2 c uncooked					
(approximate values)	—	300	6	40	15
Crackers, rye wafers, 2	13	45	2	10	Tr
Crackers, saltines, 4	11	50	1	8	1
Crackers, sea round, 1	14	60	1	10	2
Currants, 1 c	144	408	6	107	Tr
Custard, 1 c	265	305	14	29	15
Dates, chopped, 1/4 c	—	130	1	31	0
Dates, dried, 10 dates	83	228	2	61	Tr
Dates, pitted, 1 c	178	490	4	130	1
Egg, 1	50	80	6	Tr	6
Egg, whole, dried, 2 T	10	62	5	Tr	4
Falafel, 1 c dry mix	—	516	32	80	8
Figs, dried, 1	21	60	1	15	Tr
Flour, all-purpose, 1 T	7	26	1	6	Tr
Flour, all-purpose, 1 c	115	420	12	88	1
Flour, buckwheat, light, 1 c	98	340	6	78	1
Flour, whole wheat, 1 c	120	400	16	85	2
Fruit, dehydrated, mixed,					
1/4 c (approx 2 oz)	57	150	1	39	1
Fruit roll-ups, 1 roll	15	50	0	12	1
Fruitcake, dark, 1 slice	30	110	2	4	18
Gingerbread, 1 piece	63	175	2	32	4
Granola, 2 oz (from store)	57	260	6	36	10
Granola bars, oat & honey, 2	47	240	4	34	10
Honey, 1 t	7	22	Tr	9	0
Honey, 1 T	21	65	Tr	17	0
Honey, 1 c	336	1024	2	277	0
Jams and preserves, 1 T	20	55	Tr	14	Tr
Kasha (buckwheat), 1/2 c					
uncooked	—	290	6	60	0
Lentils, 1/2 c dry	182	310	22	52	2
Lemonade, from powder	—	82	0	21	0

(Continued on next page)

Nutritive Values *(continued)*

	Weight (grams)	Calories	Protein (grams)	Carbohydrate (grams)	Fat (grams)
Macaroni, 2 oz dry (1/2 c uncooked)	57	210	8	42	1
Macaroni, 3 oz dry	86	315	11	63	2
Margarine, 1 T	14	100	0	0	12
Margarine, 1 c	224	1600	0	0	192
Milk, condensed, sweetened, 1 c	306	980	25	166	27
Milk, dry, nonfat instant, 1/3 c (makes 1 c)	23	82	8	12	Tr
Milk, dry, nonfat instant, 1 c	69	246	24	36	1
Milk, dry, nonfat instant, 1-1/3 c (makes 1 qt)	88	319	31	46	1
Milk, dry, whole, 1/4 c (makes 1 c)	32	159	8	12	9
Milk, whole, 1 c	244	160	9	12	9
Millet, 1/2 c uncooked	66	216	7	48	2
Miso, 0.3 oz (to make 8 oz soup)	9	35	3	3	1
Molasses, blackstrap, 1 T	20	45	0	11	0
Muesli, 2 oz (from store)	57	212	6	40	5
Muffin, English, 1 plain	57	135	5	26	1
Mushrooms, 1/2 c pieces raw (2 T dehydrated)	—	9	1	2	Tr
Noodles, 2 oz dry (makes 1 c prepared)	57	220	8	40	3
Noodles, 3 oz dry (makes 1.5 c prepared)	86	330	11	60	5
Oatmeal, instant (1.25 oz packet)	36	138	5	23	3
Oatmeal, instant w/apples & cinnamon	36	140	3	27	2
Oats, quick and old-fashioned, 1/3 c (1 oz)	28	100	5	18	2
Oats, 1 c	84	300	15	54	6
Oil, cooking, 1 t	5	42	0	0	5
Oil, cooking, 1 T	14	125	0	0	14
Oil, cooking, 1 c	220	1945	0	0	220
Onions, 1 medium (1/2 c chopped raw or 1/3 c dehydrated)	—	27	1	6	0
Onion flakes, 1/4 c dehydrated	14	45	1	12	Tr
Onion soup, dehydrated, 1-1/2 oz package	43	150	6	23	5

(Continued on next page)

Nutritive Values *(continued)*

	Weight (grams)	Calories	Protein (grams)	Carbohydrate (grams)	Fat (grams)
Oranges, raw, 1	180	65	1	16	Tr
Pancakes, 1 4-inch diameter	27	60	2	9	2
Peaches, raw, 1	114	35	1	10	Tr
Peaches, dried, 10 halves	130	311	5	80	1
Peaches, dried, uncooked, 1 c	160	420	5	109	1
Peanuts, roasted, scant 1/4 c (1 oz)	28	168	7	5	14
Peanuts, roasted, 1 c (about 5 oz)	144	840	37	27	72
Peanut butter, 1 T	16	95	4	3	8
Peanut butter, 1 c	256	1520	64	48	128
Pears, raw, 1 (5–7 rings dehydrated)	—	100	1	25	1
Pears, dried, 10 halves	175	459	3	122	1
Peas, green, 1 c (scant 1/2 c dehydrated)	—	115	9	19	1
Peas, split, 1/2 c dry (8 oz)	227	350	24	63	1
Peppers, green, 1 (2-1/2 to 3 T dehydrated)	—	15	1	4	Tr
Pita pocket, 1	38	106	4	21	1
Popcorn, popped, 1 c	6	25	1	5	Tr
Potatoes, 1 medium, raw (dehydrated: 1/2 c diced or 20–25 slices)	—	90	3	21	Tr
Potatoes, instant mashed, 1/3 c dry (for 1/2 c serving)	20	70	2	16	0
Pretzels, thin, twisted, 1	6	25	1	5	Tr
Prunes, dried, 4	32	70	1	18	Tr
Pudding, chocolate, 1 c	260	385	8	67	12
Raisins, seedless, 1/2 c (packed)	83	240	2	64	Tr
Raisins, seedless, 1 c (packed)	165	480	4	128	Tr
Rice, brown, 1/2 c uncooked	—	232	5	50	1
Rice, brown, instant, 1/2 c uncooked	53	180	4	42	1
Rice, creamed, 5 T (2 oz)	57	200	4	46	0
Rice, white, 1/2 c uncooked	—	225	4	50	1
Rice, wild, 1/2 c uncooked	80	283	12	61	Tr
Rice cake, 1	12	42	Tr	10	Tr
Rotini, 2 oz uncooked	57	210	8	42	1
Rotini, 3 oz uncooked	86	315	11	63	2

(Continued on next page)

Nutritive Values *(continued)*

	Weight (grams)	Calories	Protein (grams)	Carbohydrate (grams)	Fat (grams)
Salami, dry, 1 oz	28	130	7	Tr	11
Salmon, canned, 3 oz	85	120	17	0	5
Sardines, 3 oz	85	175	20	0	9
Sauce, white, 1 c	250	405	10	22	31
Sausage, pork, 2 links, cooked	26	125	5	Tr	11
Sesame seeds, 1 oz (3 T)	28	161	5	7	14
Sesame butter (tahini), 1 T	15	89	3	3	8
Shortening, vegetable, 1 T	13	110	0	0	13
Shortening, vegetable, 1 c	200	1770	0	0	200
Spaghetti, regular or angel hair, 2 oz uncooked	57	210	8	42	1
Spaghetti, 3 oz uncooked	86	315	11	63	2
Soy nuts, roasted, 1/4 c	43	203	15	15	11
Soy nuts, roasted, 1/2 c	86	405	30	29	22
Sugar, white, granulated, 1 t	4	13	0	4	0
Sugar, white, granulated, 1 T	11	40	0	11	0
Sugar, white, granulated, 1 c	200	770	0	199	0
Sugar, brown, 1 T	14	51	0	13	0
Sugar, brown, 1 c packed	220	820	0	212	0
Sunflower seeds, dry roasted, 1/4 c (1 oz)	28	165	6	7	14
Sunflower seeds, dry roasted, 1 c	112	648	26	21	56
Tapioca, instant, 1 T	9	32	Tr	8	0
Tapioca cream pudding, 1 c	165	220	8	28	8
Tomatoes, 1 raw (8–12 slices dehydrated)	—	24	1	5	Tr
Tomato paste, 6 oz (about 2/3 c)	175	150	6	35	0
Tomato powder, 5 T	—	40	2	9	0
Tomato vegetable soup w/noodles, 2-1/2 oz	71	245	6	45	6
Tortellini, 1 c uncooked (approximate values)	—	210	8	42	1
Tortilla, corn, 1	30	67	2	13	1
Tortilla, flour, 1	—	85	3	15	2
Tuna, canned in water, 3 oz	85	116	23	0	2
Walnuts, chopped, scant 1/4 c (1 oz)	28	180	6	4	17
Walnuts, chopped, 1 c (about 5 oz)	126	790	26	19	75

(Continued on next page)

Nutritive Values *(continued)*

	Weight (grams)	Calories	Protein (grams)	Carbohydrate (grams)	Fat (grams)
Wheat, creamed, 1 pkt (1 oz)	28	100	3	21	1
Wheat, creamed, about 1/2 c dry	57	200	6	42	2
Wheat germ, toasted, 1 oz (3–4 T)	28	100	9	12	3
Wheat germ, toasted, 1 c	112	400	36	48	12
Zucchini, 1/2 c slices	90	14	1	4	Tr

Milford Cushman

8
Specialized Backpacking Food

Backpacking food has changed a great deal since the summer of 1972, when I lived on neon macaroni and cheese. Companies now offer dozens of all-natural dinner entrees with enticing names like Cashew Mushroom Curry, Chili Cheese Nachos, Spinach Pasta Stroganoff, Turkey & Asparagus, and Leonardo da Fettuccine. You can also order individual ingredients, from freeze-dried shitake mushrooms to powdered sour cream, to make your own entrees. One company makes mixes specifically for the BakePacker, and another makes mixes for the Outback Oven.

The following companies responded to my letter requesting information about their products. I have included representative entrees or ingredients with information on weight, cooking time, price, and nutritional contents. Although specific recipes and entrees may change over time, you can compare lists to get an overview of the type of products available and their relative merits.

Serving sizes are, in most cases, for prepared food. Values for protein, carbohydrates, and fats have been rounded to the nearest whole number. Weight is dry weight of the package contents, not the prepared weight. In some cases nutritional values were not available. Comments concerning whether a product is free of preservatives, artificial flavors and colors, and/or MSG are based on labels and company literature. I have noted when a product contains an additive (except for salt, hydrogenated vegetable oil, or forms of sugar) that the Center for Science in the Public Interest (CSPI) recommends avoiding or using with caution. I have also noted when a product contains hydrolyzed vegetable protein, autolyzed yeast or yeast extract, or additives that contain MSG.

"Add b. water" means that to prepare a product, boiling water must be added to it—no cooking is required. There is a trade-off when you use "instant" food. What you gain in time, you lose in texture. Paper-thin noodles, for example, cook quickly but do not provide the firmness that longer-cooking noodles do. As you choose trip food, keep in mind your needs concerning fuel, weight, nutrition, and so on, and choose accordingly.

Adventure Foods
Route 2, Box 276
Whittier, NC 28789
(704) 497-4113

Offers sixteen dinner entrees, sixteen BakePacker mixes, and several dozen individual ingredients; also offers soy protein with various meat flavors, jerky, pemmican bars, and instant soups. The product list includes powdered versions of hard-to-pack ingredients like honey, molasses, shortening, soy sauce, vinegar, and Worcestershire sauce. The list also includes unusual items like dehydrated cherries, dehydrated cranberries, and instant sweet potatoes. Adventure Foods has published a cookbook of recipes for the BakePacker. You can mail-order any of the items; shipping is extra. Some products are available at outdoor stores. The products listed below are designed for the Standard (7-inch) BakePacker; mixes for the Ultralight BakePacker are also available.

Product	Serv per pkg	Serv size	Weight	Cooking time	Price	Cal	Pro Gm	Car Gm	Fat Gm
Blueberry Muffin Mix (also pancake mix)	4	1/4 of 7" round	295 g (10.4 oz)	20–25 min	$3.95	215	5	4	39
Chocolate cake	4	1/4 cake	273 g (9.6 oz)	15 min	$4.95	462	7	81	12
Gingerbread[1]	4	1/4 cake	199 g (7 oz)	25 min	$3.49	189	3	43	1
Honey Cornbread[1]	4	1/4 pkg	273 g (9.6 oz)	20 min	$2.95	253	5	54	2
Indian Beanbread[1]	4	1/4 pkg	295 g (10.4 oz)	20–25 min	$3.69	303	8	54	6
Deepdish Pizza[2]	4	1/4 pizza	295 g (10.4 oz)	15 min	$7.69	300	10	53	5
If used for two	2	1/2 pizza				601	20	107	11

[1]These products contain sodium aluminum phosphate, an ingredient in baking powder that the CSPI recommends using with caution.

[2]The cheese spread in this product contains artificial colors, which the CSPI recommends using with caution or avoiding altogether.

Comments:

The mixes bake up nicely. Except for the pizza, all you have to do is add water, mix, and bake. The pizza mix is a clever adaptation of an at-home favorite, but I suggest skipping the cheese spread and taking along a small chunk of mozzarella.

AlpineAire
P.O. Box 1600
Nevada City, CA 95959
1 (800) 322-6325

Offers thirty-five dinner entrees plus side dishes, soups, fruits, desserts, and breakfasts. A wide variety of individual ingredients, such as beans, grains, meat, vegetables, dairy products, and fruits are available in bulk. Most AlpineAire products are freeze-dried, though some are dehydrated or powdered. The company carries gourmet items like freeze-dried shitake mushrooms. All foods are free of preservatives, MSG, and artificial flavors or colors.

AlpineAire sells entrees through retail stores and all of its products through mail-order. The company pays for shipping on orders over twenty-five dollars. Ask for the Outdoor Kitchen catalog.

Product	Serv per pkg	Serv size	Weight	Cooking time	Price	Cal	Pro Gm	Car Gm	Fat Gm
Entrees									
Leonardo da Fettucine	2	1-1/3 c	155 g (5.5 oz)	Add b. water	$4.99	295	15	45	3
Santa Fe Black Beans & Rice	2	1-1/2 c	184 g (6.5 oz)	Add b. water	$4.99	Not available			
Summer Chicken	2	1-1/3 c	155 g (5.5 oz)	Add b. water	$5.98	Not available			
Turkey Romanoff	2	1-1/3 c	155 g (5.5 oz)	Add b. water	$5.98	Not available			
Blueberry Honey Granola w/Almonds & Milk	2	3/4 c	184 g (6.5 oz)	None	$2.85	367	15	54	11
5-Grain Fruit Nut Instant Cereal	2	1-1/2 c	141 g (5 oz)	Add b. water	$2.10	Not available			
Individual Ingredients									
Eggs, Scrambling & Omelette Egg Mix (2 T = 1 egg)	6	4 eggs	12 oz	—	$5.98	77	5	3	5
Tomato Powder	12	1/2 c sauce	8 oz	—	$4.95	40	2	9	0
Cheddar Cheese Powder	4	1/2 c	8 oz	—	$5.95	164	11	1	14
Sour Cream Powder	4	1/2 c	8 oz	—	$3.95	215	3	50	0

Note:
AlpineAire recommends using all ingredients within thirty days of opening the package. It is possible to extend the shelf life somewhat by putting the product in a reclosable bag and storing it in the freezer.

Comments:

AlpineAire's products are uniformly high in quality. The tomato powder makes excellent sauce. The turkey in Turkey Romanoff tastes like real turkey and the asparagus in Summer Chicken is heavenly. The entrees are quick and easy to prepare. Even someone who does not know how to cook can get good results.

AlpineAire has the widest variety of entrees and ingredients of all the companies I reviewed. The mail-order service is excellent.

Backpacker's Pantry
6350 Gunpark Drive
Boulder, CO 80301
(303) 581-5018

Offers twenty-six dinner entrees plus breakfasts, snacks, fruits, vegetables, desserts, and freeze-dried meats and jerky. You can mail-order any item; shipping is extra. If you want an item that is not in your local store, request that it be ordered from the company. You can get a catalog, a list of ingredients, and a list of dealers from the manufacturer. Nutritional information for all products is not available at this time.

Company literature states: "Preservatives are added in trace amounts to some of our ingredients to prevent discoloration and flavor loss during processing. They aren't added to extend storage life. Most of our items don't use any preservatives. All our products are MSG free."

Product	Serv per pkg	Serv size	Weight	Cooking time	Price	Cal	Pro Gm	Car Gm	Fat Gm
Denver Omelette[1]	2	3.75 oz	80 g (2.75 oz)	Until done	$2.60	177	19	7	9
Butter	4	4.5 t	85 g (3 oz)	None	$2.60	250			
Freeze-dried Pears[2]	2	.25 oz	21 g (.5 oz)	None	$1.60	27	0	5	0
Freeze-dried IceCream[1]	2	.31 oz	14 g (.75 oz)	None	$2.30	Not available			
Chili Cheese Nachos	2	12 oz	255 g (9 oz)	Add b. water	$5.95	Not available			

(Continued on next page)

Product	Serv per pkg	Serv size	Weight	Cooking time	Price	Cal	Pro Gm	Car Gm	Fat Gm
Black Bean Tamale Pie	2	12 oz	262 g (9.25 oz)	Add b. water	$5.50	Not available			
Santa Fe Chicken	2	12 oz	227 g (8 oz)	Add b. water	$7.50	Not available			
Green Beans Almondine	2	2 oz	21 g (.75 oz)	Add b. water	$1.90	Not available			
Peaches & Cream Pie[1]	2	6 oz	128 g (4.5 oz)	None	$3.00	Not available			
Apple Cobbler[1]	2	6 oz	142 g (5 oz)	15 min	$2.35	Not available			
Coffee Bags	5 bags			Add b. water	$1.90				

[1]Contains artificial flavors, artificial colors, and/or other additives that the Center for Science in the Public Interest recommends using with caution or avoiding altogether.
[2]Contains sulfite; CSPI recommends avoiding sulfiting agents.
Note: 12 fluid ounces equals 1-1/2 cups.

Comments:

Santa Fe Chicken gets top marks on taste. Chili Cheese Nachos and Black Bean Tamale Pie also get high ratings; the tortilla chips included in the entree add the kind of crunch and flavor you do not otherwise get on trail. Apple Cobbler is good but very sweet. The packets of butter and coffee bags are handy for a trip when you do not want to carry a pantry. The astronauts can have Freeze-dried IceCream. One-half ounce (21 g) of freeze-dried pears has 54 calories and costs $1.60, while one large piece of dried pear (18 g) has 46 calories and costs far less. In this case, dried fruit is a better deal; it tastes better, too.

Harvest Foodworks
66 Victoria Avenue, Smiths Falls
Ontario, Canada K7A 2P4
1 (800) 268-4268

Offers twelve dinner entrees plus breakfasts, desserts, vegetables, and side dishes. Company literature states: "No artificial preservatives, flavors, or colors." No meat or meat products are used. Ingredient lists are not currently available, but the company plans to publish listings in the future. Entrees come in two-person, four-person,

and six-person sizes. If you live in the United States, order
from one of the three suppliers listed after the chart.

Product	Serv per pkg	Serv size	Weight	Cooking time	Price	Cal	Pro Gm	Car Gm	Fat Gm
Scrambled Egg Mix	2	3/4 c	81 g (2.8 oz)	Until done	$4.98	230	18	1	16
Flapjacks & Syrup	2	Four 4" pancakes	339 g (11.8 oz)	Until done	$3.98	713	14	136	5
Big Bill's Multigrain Cereal			301 g		$3.15	587	18	115	6
Hot	2	2.6 c	(10.6 oz)	5 min					
Cold	2	1.4 c		None					
Corn Biscuits & Applesauce	2	Two 4" biscuits	233 g (7.8 oz)	Until done	$4.15	447	16	76	9
Bannock Bread Mix	2	One 8" loaf	378 g (13.3 oz)	Until done	$3.15	576	15	126	2
Powdered Shortening (1 T powdered = 2 T whole)	5 T	1 T	50 g (1.8 oz)	—	$1.98	455			50
Alfredo Primavera[2]	2	1-3/4 c	216 g (7.6 oz)	12 min	$6.82	454	19	58	17
Couscous Almondine[2]	2	1-3/4 c	273 g (9.6 oz)	12 min	$6.42	536	27	78	15
Big Bill's Beans & Rice[2]	2	1-3/4 c	249 g (8.7 oz)	15 min	$6.82	425	20	84	1
Mediterranean Pasta[2]	2	1-3/4 c	237 g (8.3 oz)	15 min	$6.42	396	27	73	2
Stroganoff w/Wine Sauce[2]	2	1-3/4 c	246 g (8.6 oz)	12 min	$6.82	445	25	72	8
Oriental Sweet & Sour[2]	2	1-3/4 c	310 g (10.9 oz)	15 min	$6.42	554	26	106	5
Corn w/Butter Sauce	2	3/4 c	67 g (2.3 oz)	5 min	$3.82	107	4	21	1
Peas & Onions w/Butter	2	3/4 c	62 g (2.1 oz)	5 min	$3.82	111	6	21	1
Apple & Walnut Coffee Cake	2	Half of 10" cake	221 g (7.7 oz)	Until done	$3.32	224	5	42	5
Blueberry Cobbler	2	Half of 8" cake	155 g (5.5 oz)	13 min	$3.48	316	5	60	7
Chocolate Chew Cookies[1]	2	Five 2" cookies	280 g (9.8 oz)	None	$3.32	679	10	92	30
Coconut Snackaroons	2	Six 1" cookies	158 g (5.5 oz)	None	$2.65	382	6	53	16

[1]Contains sodium metabisulfite; CSPI recommends avoiding this additive.

[2]Contains yeast extract, autolyzed yeast extract, hydrolyzed plant protein, or natural flavor enhancer (which may contain yeast extract); see note regarding MSG in Chapter 2.

Comments:

The portions for dinners are quite generous, a hefty 1-3/4
cups per person. (Big Bill's Cereal, when cooked, makes
over 2-1/2 cups per person.) The dinners require more
preparation than do those of other companies. The
dinners also require some cooking, but they have "real
food" texture that you cannot get with instant, no-cook

food. The packages include a calibrated paper cup so you can add the correct amount of water. The Flapjacks are tasty: the syrup contains turbinado sugar and maple sugar granules. Big Bill's Beans & Rice is well worth stirring the pot for fifteen minutes. Alfredo Primavera gets a high rating, too; it has a nice, creamy sauce, and the colored noodles provide eye appeal. The Stroganoff and Mediterranean Pasta are fair; the gravy-brown color of the Stroganoff is not appealing. It took me a while to figure out that the puzzling gray ingredient in the dinners is textured vegetable protein. Beware the MSG in the entrees. The main attribute of the no-cook coconut cookies is that they are sweet.

I used the powdered shortening in several baking mixes, all of which turned out nicely. Powdered shortening can also be used to grease a pan for eggs or pancakes. It is expensive but handy.

These three U.S. companies distribute Harvest Foodworks products by mail: Campmor, Box 997-V, Paramus, NJ, 1 (800) 526-4784 (orders only), (201) 445-9868 (NJ residents only); The Boundary Waters Catalogue, Piragis Northwoods Co., 105 N. Central Avenue, Ely, MN 55731, 1 (800) 223-6565; The Food Cache, Box 7, Waterford, WI 53185, 1 (800) 526-1704.

Mountain House
Oregon Freeze Dry
P.O. Box 1048
Albany, OR 97321
(503) 926-6001

Offers seventeen dinner entrees (none of which are vegetarian) plus vegetables, breakfasts, and snacks. Oregon Freeze Dry does not offer mail-order, but its products can be mail-ordered from Recreational Equipment, Inc., Mail Order Department, 1700 45th Street East, Sumner, WA 98325, 1 (800) 426-4840, and other retailers. Lists of ingredients and distributors are available from Oregon Freeze Dry.

Products are advertised as containing "no preservatives" and "no artificial ingredients." However, see comments below.

Product	Serv per pkg	Serv size	Weight	Cooking time	Price	Cal	Pro Gm	Car Gm	Fat Gm
Chicken Polynesian[3]	2	1 c	99 g (3.5 oz)	Add b. water	$4.99	210	10	33	4
Beef & Rice w/Green Pepper & Onion Sauce[3]	2	1 c	108 g (3.8 oz)	Add b. water	$4.99	230	10	32	7
Beef Stew[1 & 3]	2	1 c	95 g (3.35 oz)	Add b. water	$4.49	260	16	26	9
Turkey Tetrazzini[3]	2	1 c	91 g (3.2 oz)	Add b. water	$4.99	210	13	21	8
Fruit Crisps: Peaches[2]	2	1/4 c	31 g (1.1 oz)	None	$2.49	60	0	15	0
Fruit Crisps: Pears[2]	2	1/4 c	28 g (1 oz)	None	$2.49	60	0	14	0

[1]Contains monosodium glutamate, rated "caution" by CSPI.
[2]Contains sodium bisulfite, a preservative, rated "avoid" by CSPI.
[3]Contains hydrolyzed vegetable protein, hydrolyzed plant protein, yeast extract, and/or autolyzed yeast; see note regarding MSG in Chapter 2.

Comments:

These entrees are old-style freeze-dried food with heavy cornstarch thickening and a lot of salt. The 1-cup portions are on the small side. "Cut and formed pieces" of Fruit Crisps means that the fruit is mixed with sugar and then reformulated into lightweight, light-colored, brittle chunks that melt in your mouth. It's an expensive way to get fruit: for $2.49, you get 1/2 cup of pieces that contains 60 calories.

Natural High
Richmoor Corp.
P.O. Box 8092
Van Nuys, CA 91409
(818) 787-2510

Natural High is Richmoor's "gourmet camping" line. It includes twenty-three dinner entrees (including meatless entrees) plus soups, desserts, and vegetables. Company literature states: "Free of preservatives, additives, artificial colors and flavors."

Product	Serv per pkg	Serv size	Weight	Cooking time	Price	Cal	Pro Gm	Car Gm	Fat Gm
Mexican Omelette	2	1/2 c	106 g (3.75 oz)	Until done	$2.59	Not available			
Shrimp Cantonese	2	1-1/4 c	142 g (5 oz)	Add b. water	$6.49	Not available			

(Continued on next page)

Product	Serv per pkg	Serv size	Weight	Cooking time	Price	Cal	Pro Gm	Car Gm	Fat Gm
Zucchini Lasagna	2	1-1/4 c	120 g (4.25 oz)	Add b. water	$5.49		Not available		
Fettucine Primavera	2	1-1/4 c	127 g (4.5 oz)	Add b. water	$5.49		Not available		
Corn	2	1/4 c	28 g (1 oz)	Add b. water	$1.69		Not available		
Chocolate Fudge Mousse	2	3/4 c	142 g (5 oz)	None	$2.89		Not available		
Strawberry Mousse	2	3/4 c	120 g (4.25 oz)	None	$2.89		Not available		

Comments:
The Mexican Omelette is spicy without being hot, and the tortilla chips add a nice crunchy texture. Shrimp Cantonese has tiny, delicious shrimp and a good flavor. This dish, too, is spicy but not hot. Zucchini Lasagna does not resemble lasagna in the least. The vegetables in Fettucine Primavera add color but not much to the taste. Strawberry Mousse gets much higher marks than the Chocolate Fudge Mousse, even though they have a similar base. If the Chocolate Fudge Mousse had been called Quick Chocolate Pudding I would have been more satisfied.

Traveling Light, Inc.
1563 Solano Avenue, Suite 284
Berkeley, CA 94707
(510) 526-8401

Offers mixes for pizza, quiche, coffee cake, apple pie, carrot cake, fudge brownies, banana nut bread, scones, cornbread, and Italian pan bread to be used with the Outback Oven, which is 9 inches around. The mixes range in price from $6.55 for Pizza Pesto to $3.65 for Fudge Brownies to $3.25 for Scones. The company also makes and sells the oven and various accessories. Items are available through mail-order and from retailers across the country.

Comments:

As this book is being written, Traveling Light is reformulating its mixes. According to the company, the mixes will contain whole unbleached flour, canola oil, and no preservatives or artificial ingredients. I have not tested any of the new mixes. Even with a white-flour crust, the old-recipe Pizza Pesto was outstanding. These mixes are clearly aimed at the gourmet market.

Uncle John's Foods
P.O. Box 489
Fairplay, CO 80440
1 (800) 530-8733

Offers ten entrees plus two salads; products do not contain red meat, fish, or chicken. All entrees are cooked and then air-dried; salads are air-dried. Uncle John's Foods are available through mail-order only. Prices include shipping and handling.

Product	Serv per pkg	Serv size	Weight[1]	Cooking time[2]	Price	Cal	Pro Gm	Car Gm	Fat Gm
London Fog Pea Soup	2	1 to 1-1/2 c	227 g (8 oz)	Soak & heat	$6.00	Not available			
Curried Vegetables w/Couscous	2	1 to 1-1/2 c	230 g (8.1 oz)	Soak & heat	$6.00	Not available			
Desert Ratatouille w/Rice	2	1 to 1-1/2 c	210 g (7.4 oz)	Soak & heat	$6.00	Not available			
Reddy Spageddi (spaghetti w/sauce)	2	1 to 1-1/2 c	284 g (10 oz)	Soak & heat	$6.00	Not available			
Homeboy Posole	2	1 to 1-1/2 c	261 g (9.2 oz)	Soak & heat	$6.00	Not available			
Cuban Black Beans w/Rice	2	1 to 1-1/2 c	272 g (9.6 oz)	Soak & heat	$6.00	Not available			
Cowboy Chili (w/macaroni)	2	1 to 1-1/2 c	210 g (7.4 oz)	Soak & heat	$6.00	Not available			
Flying Burritos (beans w/salsa, tortillas not inc.)	2	1 to 1-1/2 c	221 g (7.8 oz)	Soak & heat	$6.00	Not available			
Wild Wild Rice (wild rice w/vegetables)	2	1 to 1-1/2 c	176 g (6.2 oz)	Soak & heat	$6.00	Not available			
Dancing Vegetables w/Barley	2	1 to 1-1/2 c	244 g (8.6 oz)	Soak & heat	$6.00	Not available			
Carrot Salad	2	—	68 g (2.4 oz)	Soak	$4.00	Not available			
Cool Hand Cuke's Salad	2	—	90 g (3.2 oz)	Soak	$4.00	Not available			

[1]Weight may vary slightly because ingredients are measured by volume.

[2]For best results, soak dehydrated food for an hour or two (the time varies somewhat per entree) and heat to taste. Company literature suggests putting dried food plus water in a reclosable plastic bag at the top of your pack so it's ready to heat at meal time. You can also simply add water and simmer until done.

Comments:

It is amazing how all those little vegetables, beans, and grains rehydrate into real food with real-food color, flavor, and texture. Desert Ratatouille, Flying Burritos, and Homeboy Posole are winners. Cowboy Chili and Cuban Black Beans are a bit bland and could use some salsa to pep them up. The salads are fresh-tasting and crunchy. These products are low-tech (air dried) and a real change from other prepackaged trail food. The ingredients are vegetables and grains that I use in my own kitchen.

9
Foods Available in Supermarkets, Health-Food Stores, and from Mail-Order Companies

This list includes products I found in my local supermarket or health-food store, and products from companies that distribute "health foods" regionally or nationally. This list does not, by any means, include every all-natural brand or product available locally or nationally.

Serving sizes are given as they appear on the package. Since many mixes are designed for use as side dishes, it is useful to look at the calorie count on the package when gauging portions for the trail. I typically use a six-serving-box mix for two people.

Nutritional information is per serving for the product as prepared according to directions. Many of the dinner mixes that call for oil can be made without this ingredient; the fat, however, is useful on trail for boosting calories. Unless otherwise specified, weight is the dry weight of the package contents.

Comments concerning whether a product is organic or free of preservatives are from company literature.

Fractions have been rounded to the nearest whole number.

"Tr" means that the nutrient is present in trace quantities; @ is an abbreviation for "approximately."

The baking and pancake mixes from these companies were uniformly good. With a few exceptions, like buckwheat pancakes and jalapeño cornbread, I would probably not be able to tell the different brands apart in a blind test. I have therefore not made detailed comments on these products.

Annie's Homegrown, Inc.
11 Sea Avenue
Quincy, MA 02169
(617) 786-9366

Annie's Homegrown offers these mixes, plus popcorn. The company is expanding its distribution, so if these products are not in your store, ask the manager to stock them.

Product	Serv per pkg	Serv size	Weight	Cooking time	Price	Cal	Pro Gm	Car Gm	Fat Gm
Annie's Shells & Cheddar	4	@3/4 c	206 g (7.25 oz)	6–8 min	$ .99	300	8	34	15
Annie's Whole Wheat Shells & Cheddar	4	@3/4 c	206 g (7.25 oz)	6–8 min	$1.09	300	8	43	15
Annie's Alfredo w/Garlic & Garden Basil	4	@3/4 c	206 g (7.25 oz)	6–8 min	$ .99	240	8	34	10

Comments:

Tasty, easy to prepare, inexpensive, and made with real ingredients as opposed to chemicals. This is not *real* mac and cheese (or Alfredo), but it is the best dry-mix version I have found.

Arrowhead Mills
Box 2059
Hereford, TX 79045
(806) 364-0730

Arrowhead Mills has a wide selection of grains, beans, seeds, nut and seed butters, oils, hot and cold cereals, flours, and mixes. Many of the products are organically grown. Arrowhead Mills products are sold in health-food stores and some supermarkets, but they are also available by mail-order. Write the company for a full list of products and prices. There is a shipping and handling charge.

Product	Serv per pkg	Serv size	Weight	Cooking time	Price	Cal	Pro Gm	Car Gm	Fat Gm
Bear Mush	22	1 oz uncooked	623 g (22 oz)	2–3 min	$1.05	100	3	21	0
7 Grain Cereal	24	1 oz uncooked	680 g (24 oz)	15 min	$1.70	100	4	17	1
Multigrain Pancake & Waffle Mix	11	1/2 c (four 5" cakes)	907 g (32 oz)	Until done	$2.25	290	11	58	2
Quick Brown Rice w/Wild Rice & Herbs	4	1.3 oz	151 g (5.35 oz)	15 min	$1.79	140	4	28	1
Potato Flakes	4	2 oz	227 g (8 oz)	Add b. water	$1.11	140	5	44	0

Product Notes:
The Multigrain Pancake mix does not require additional ingredients. Potato Flakes require butter and milk, and the flakes themselves are from organically grown potatoes.

Comments:
The products are consistently good. I was delighted to find, finally, potato flakes without additives, and I used these flakes in my instant soup recipes. The Quick Brown Rice mix contains brown rice, wild rice, soy sauce powder, and herbs; it is fairly quick to prepare and quite delicious.

Bear Valley
Intermountain Trading Company, Ltd.
P.O. Box 6157
Albany, CA 94706-0157
(510) 526-3623

Intermountain Trading Company makes four different high-calorie, high-protein bars under the brand name of Bear Valley. These products are distributed through health-food stores and outdoor stores. Contact the company for further information if the products are not available in your area.

Product	Serv per pkg	Serv size	Weight	Cooking time	Price	Cal	Pro Gm	Car Gm	Fat Gm
Carob-cocoa Pemmican Bar	1	1 bar	106 g (3.75 oz)	—	$1.05 to 1.30	440	16	68	12
Fruit 'n Nut Pemmican Bar	1	1 bar	106.4 g (3.75 oz)	—	Same	420	17	59	13

Product Notes:
The amino acids in the pemmican bars are complemented to produce complete protein; the bars do not contain meat.

Comments:
The bars are great mini-meals. You get a lot of calories plus a significant amount of protein (one-third of the daily protein requirement for women and over one-fourth for men). The bars I sampled taste good and have a nice baked texture that is quite different from caramel-type bars that threaten to take out your fillings. They are also handy and easy to carry in your day pack or your pocket.

Brumwell Milling
123 East 1st Street
Sumner, IA 50674
(319) 578-8106

Brumwell sells flour, cereals, and mixes for baked goods. The company uses grains grown without chemical pesticides. These baking mixes can be ordered through the mail; shipping and handling are extra.

Product	Cups per pkg	Serv size	Weight	Cooking time	Price	Cal	Pro Gm	Car Gm	Fat Gm
Pancake & Waffle Mix	@5	1/2 c mix	680 g (24 oz)	Until done	$1.69		Not available		
Whole Wheat Pancake Mix	@5	1/2 c mix	680 g (24 oz)	Until done	$1.69		Not available		
Buckwheat Pancake Mix	@5	1/2 c mix	680 g (24 oz)	Until done	$1.75		Not available		
Gourmet Biscuit Mix	@3	1/4 c mix	397 g (14 oz)	10–12 min	$1.19		Not available		
Corn Bread Mix	@2	1/4 c mix (8" pan)	284 g (10 oz)	20–25 min	$1.19		Not available		

Product Notes:
The Corn Bread Mix requires egg and oil. The other mixes listed can be made with either water or milk.

Comments:
The mixes are uniformly delicious. The cornbread made up well with powdered eggs and powdered shortening. The buckwheat pancakes were a real hit.

Eden Foods
701 Tecumseh Road
Clinton, MI 49236
(517) 456-7424

Eden Foods sells organic pasta, organic whole grains and dry beans, seasonings, and a variety of Japanese foods.

Product	Serv per pkg	Serv size	Weight	Cooking time	Price	Cal	Pro Gm	Car Gm	Fat Gm
Dried Tofu	6 small blocks		165 g (5.8 oz)	soak in hot water	—		Not available		
Parsley Garlic Ribbons	4	2 oz	226 g (8 oz)	5–8 min	$1.99	230	8	44	Tr
Edensoy Organic Soy Beverage	1	8.45 fl oz	250 ml	—	—	140	10	14	4

Comments:
Tofu does not survive the freeze-drying process; rehydrated tofu is rubbery and unappealing. I found that the

flavor of Parsley Garlic Ribbons was so delicate that it was overwhelmed by the sauce I used. The soy beverage is useful for people who cannot drink milk, but because it is liquid, you wind up carrying around extra weight.

Erewhon
U.S. Mills
395 Elliot Street
Newton Upper Falls, MA 02164
(617) 969-5400

Erewhon offers a variety of cold and hot cereals, nut and seed butters, and Japanese products.

Product	Serv per pkg	Serv size	Weight	Cooking time	Price	Cal	Pro Gm	Car Gm	Fat Gm
Honey Almond Granola	16	scant 1/4 c	454 g (16 oz)	None	$2.99	130	3	17	6
Instant Oatmeal: Maple Spice	8	1 pkt (@1/2 c)	272 g (9.6 oz)	Add b. water	$2.79	140	4	24	3
Instant Oatmeal: Apple Cinnamon	8	1 pkt (@1/2 c)	280 g (9.9 oz)	Add b. water	$2.79	145	4	25	3

Comments:
This brand is the only instant oatmeal I have found that is not packed with sugar; the sweeteners—used moderately—are maple syrup and fruit. The granola is good, too.

Fantastic Foods
106 Galli Drive
Petaluma, CA 94954
(707) 778-7801

Fantastic Foods carries a wide variety of grain, bean, and vegetable products, including falafel, couscous, potatoes au gratin, quick pilafs, soups, and pasta salads. Fantastic Foods products are widely available in supermarkets.

Product	Serv per pkg	Serv size	Weight	Cooking time	Price	Cal	Pro Gm	Car Gm	Fat Gm
Vegetarian Chili Mix* (beans not included)	14	1/2 c	182 g (6.4 oz)	25 min	$1.79	104	8	19	1

(Continued on next page)

Product	Serv per pkg	Serv size	Weight	Cooking time	Price	Cal	Pro Gm	Car Gm	Fat Gm
Quick Brown Rice Pilaf	5	1/2 c	140 g (5 oz)	12 min	$1.69	96	2	21	1
Mandarin Chow Mein* (tofu not included)	6	1/2 c	113 g (4 oz)	7 min	$1.79	134	8	14	9
Macaroni & Cheese	5	1/2 c	142 g (5 oz)	6–8 min	$1.69	112	5	19	2
Nature's Burger (1-1/2 c mix)	7–10 patties		284 g (10 oz)	Add b. water; fry patties	$1.79	152	7	21	4
Tabouli Salad Mix	8	1/2 c	170 g (6 oz)	No cooking	$1.69	161	2	17	10
Instant Refried Beans	5	1/2 c	200 g (7 oz)	Add b. water	$1.79	136	8	23	1
Instant Black Beans	4	1/2 c	200 g (7 oz)	Add b. water	$1.79	136	8	23	1
Hummus Mix	8	1/4 c	170 g (6 oz)	No cooking	$1.79	111	4	10	7
Potatoes Au Gratin	5	1/2 c	155 g (5.5 oz)	30 min	$1.69	156	6	25	4

*Contains hydrolyzed vegetable protein; see note regarding MSG in Chapter 2.

Product Notes:

The nutritional values are for the product as prepared per instructions, even if the instructions call for additional ingredients. Vegetarian Chili calls for beans, Mandarin Chow Mein calls for tofu and oil, Macaroni & Cheese and Potatoes Au Gratin call for milk and (optional) butter; Tabouli calls for oil and tomatoes. For other products, oil or butter is optional.

Comments:

The instant refries, black beans, and hummus are extremely handy. The chili is quite tasty and would be good over rice or with beans. The Potatoes Au Gratin mix is the only such supermarket mix I have located that does not have additives. The remaining products I found to be fair to good but not outstanding. Mandarin Chow Mein and Macaroni & Cheese are both on the salty side. The cheese sauce in the macaroni is runny, orangish, and unappealing. I prefer falafel burgers to Nature's Burger.

**Fearn Natural Foods and Gayelord Hauser
Divisions of Modern Products, Inc.
P.O. Box 09398
Milwaukee, WI 53209
(414) 352-3209**

Fearn Natural Foods offers a variety of cake, pancake, and muffin mixes; soup and stew mixes; vegetarian burger mixes; and other natural foods. The Gayelord Hauser division offers almost a dozen all-natural seasonings.

Product	Serv per pkg	Serv size	Weight	Cooking time	Price	Cal	Pro Gm	Car Gm	Fat Gm
Whole Wheat Baking Mix (5-1/4 c mix)	9.7	1/2 c mix	737 g (26 oz)	—	$2.99	220	10	46	2
Corn Bread Mix (2 c mix = 8" pan)	6	1/6 pan	270 g (9.5 oz)	25–30 min	$1.49	147	5	27	2
Banana Cake Mix (2 c mix = 8" cake)	6	1/6 cake	244 g (8.6 oz)	30–35 min	$2.19	130	5	26	2
Carrot Cake Mix (2 c mix = 8" cake)	6	1/6 cake	244 g (8.6 oz)	35–40 min	$2.19	140	6	26	2
Soya Granules	11	1/4 c	462 g (16 oz)	—	$1.49	140	22	13	0

Product notes:

The Baking Mix, which is made with nonaluminum-type baking powder, can be used for pancakes and biscuits; pancakes require egg, oil, and milk, and biscuits require milk and oil. The Corn Bread Mix and two cake mixes also call for egg, oil, honey, and (for cornbread) milk. Soya Granules can be used to increase the protein in cereals, casseroles, and baked goods.

Comments:

Fresh carrot cake is such a treat on trail that it is worth buying powdered eggs for this mix. The banana cake is good, too, although the banana taste is mild. The corn-bread turns out well in a BakePacker. The Baking Mix contains only whole wheat flour and makes very dense, whole-wheaty biscuits.

Gayelord Hauser produces a dozen seasoning products: Insanely Hot Naturally Cajun, Hot Naturally Cajun, Lemon Pepper, Vege-Sal, Milk Salt Free, Spicy Salt Free, Onion

Magic, Herbal Bouquet, Garlic Magic, Salt Free Spike, Spike, and Vegit. Spike and Vegit contain hydrolyzed vegetable protein; see note regarding MSG in Chapter 2.

Gibbs Wild Rice
RR 2 Box 124
Deer River, MN 56636
1 (800) 344-6378

Gibbs offers a variety of wild rice products, including wild rice soup mix and wild rice cereal.

Product	Serv per pkg	Serv size	Weight	Cooking time	Price[1]	Cal	Pro Gm	Car Gm	Fat Gm
Scout Brand Wild Rice	4	@2/3 c	114 g (4 oz)	45 min		99	4	21	Tr
Instant Wild Rice	4	@2/3 c	114 g (4 oz)	7–15 min		99	4	21	Tr
Instant Wild Rice Pilaf[2]	4	@3/4 c	128 g (4.5 oz)	7–15 min		Not available			
Gibbs Select Harvest (1-1/4 c mix)	—	114 grams	206 g (7.25 oz)	35 min		125	4	26	Tr
Snack Mix	2	1 oz	28 g (1 oz)	—		125	5	18	4

[1]Most Gibbs products are sold in multiple units. Ten 4-ounce packets of instant wild rice are $21.75, and four 4.5-ounce packets of instant pilaf are $11.50. One 1-pound box of regular wild rice is $8.55, and two 1-pound bags of wild rice are $12.60. Prices include shipping within the contiguous forty-eight states. If you are interested in these products, contact the company for a brochure.

[2]The pilaf seasoning packet contains MSG, BHA, and propyl gallate, all additives that the CSPI recommends using with caution or avoiding. The seasoning also includes hydrolyzed vegetable protein; see note regarding MSG in Chapter 2. The ingredients in the seasoning packet for the Select Harvest are not listed on the package.

Comments:

Wild rice has a delicious nutty flavor and it's even better on trail. The Snack Mix, a new product, is crunchy, nutty, and different from the usual trail mix.

Instant wild rice is well suited to camping because it cooks so quickly. Here's the math: 10 packets of instant wild rice times four ounces each with water makes about twenty-six cups of rice costing around eighty-four cents per cup. Treat yourself to some wild rice and give the extras away as birthday presents.

Because of the additives, I skipped the seasoning packet for the pilaf; salt and butter or an all-natural seasoning are good substitutes.

One pound of wild rice produces about eleven cups of cooked rice.

Hodgson Mill, Inc.
Box 430
Teutopolis, IL 62467
(217) 857-6491

Hodgson Mill makes hot cereals, pancake mixes, flour, cornmeal, baking mixes, pastas, and specialty products.

Product	Serv per pkg	Serv size	Weight	Cooking time	Price	Cal	Pro Gm	Car Gm	Fat Gm
Whole Wheat Insta-Bake	4	2 c dry	907 g (32 oz)	—	$1.87	283	8	45	8
Jalapeño Cornbread Mix	16	1 square	624 g (22 oz)	25 min	—	151	3	25	4
Oat Bran Buttermilk Pancake Mix (7 c mix)	56	1 4" cake	907 g (32 oz)	—	—	60	2	12	1
Buckwheat Pancake Mix (7 c mix)	56	1 4" cake	907 g (32 oz)	—	—	60	2	12	1
Oat Bran Hot Cereal	16	1/3 c	453 g (16 oz)	1 min	$1.99	108	5	18	2
Whole Wheat Shells	8	2 oz dry	340 g (12 oz)	12–14 min	$1.39	200	9	40	1
Veggie Rotini	8	2 oz dry	454 g (16 oz)	10–12 min	$1.79	210	7	41	1

Product Notes:
Biscuits require the addition of milk; pancakes require eggs and milk. Two cups of Insta-Bake makes eight to ten biscuits.

Comments:
My favorite mix is Jalapeño Cornbread with its subtle taste of hot peppers. Oat Bran Hot Cereal is a nice change from oatmeal because it does not have the gluey texture oatmeal has. Veggie Rotini, with its tomato-, beet-, and spinach-colored spirals, brightens up any meal.

Lundberg Family Farms
P.O. Box 369
Richvale, CA 95974
(916) 822-4551

This company makes a variety of rice products.

Product	Serv per pkg	Serv size	Weight	Cooking time	Price	Cal	Pro Gm	Car Gm	Fat Gm
Hot 'N Creamy Almond-Date Rice Cereal	12	@1/2 c	340 g (12 oz)	5 min	$1.55	110	2	24	1
Quick Chicken Pilaf	6	@1/2 c	170 g (6 oz)	10 min	$1.35	127	2	26	3
Quick Spanish Pilaf*	6	@1/2 c	170 g (6 oz)	10 min	$1.35	107	2	22	2
Lundberg Countrywild	—	—	454 g (16 oz)	45 min	$1.70	Not available			

*Contains hydrolyzed yeast protein; see note regarding MSG in Chapter 2.

Product Notes:
Directions for the pilaf mixes call for butter, margarine, or oil, although you can make them without the added fat.

Comments:
Quick Spanish Pilaf is great and so is the Almond-Date Rice Cereal. In fact, people who do not usually like hot cereal came back for seconds of this one. Chicken Pilaf has a mild flavor and is improved with a bit of Cheddar cheese.

Mayacamas Fine Foods, Inc.
1206 E. MacArthur
Sonoma, CA 95476
(707) 996-0955

Mayacamas makes six instant soup mixes plus non-instant dehydrated soup mixes, sauce mixes, dip mixes, and salad dressing mixes. Products are available in supermarkets and health-food stores. Mixes may also be ordered (in cartons of twelve packages) at five dollars per carton. Write for an order form.

Product	Serv per pkg	Serv size	Weight	Cooking time	Price	Cal	Pro Gm	Car Gm	Fat Gm
Instant Soup: Garden Pea*	1	3/4 c	18 g (.65 oz)	Add b. water	$.79	75	Not available		1
Instant Soup: Chicken Leek*	1	3/4 c	18 g (.65 oz)	Add b. water	$.79	75	Not available		1
Instant Soup: Black Bean*	1	3/4 c	18 g (.65 oz)	Add b. water	$.79	75	Not available		1
Instant Soup: Broccoli*	1	3/4 c	18 g (.65 oz)	Add b. water	$.79	75	Not available		1
Tomato Pesto Sauce Mix (add to 6 oz tomato paste)	—	—	31 g (1.1 oz)	—		8	Not available		1

*Contains hydrolyzed plant protein and/or autolyzed yeast; see note regarding MSG in Chapter 2.

Product Notes:
The labeling needs some attention. According to the ingredient list, the chicken soup does not contain any chicken or chicken products, and the Tomato Pesto Sauce does not contain any tomato products.

Comments:
The individual portions are handy; the soups received fair to good ratings.

Near East Food Products Co.
797 Lancaster Street
Leominster, MA 01453

Near East sells a full line of rice, lentil, and couscous mixes, plus falafel.

Product	Serv per pkg	Serv size	Weight	Cooking time	Price	Cal	Pro Gm	Car Gm	Fat Gm
Wheat Pilaf Mix*	6	1/2 c	170 g (6 oz)	15 min	$1.59	170	2	25	6
Curry Rice Mix*	6	1/2 c	177 g (6.25 oz)	25–30 min	$1.50	160	2	24	5
Rice Pilaf Mix*	6	1/2 c	173 g (6.09 oz)	25–30 min	$ .99	120	2	26	0
Spanish Rice Mix*	6	1/2 c	191 g (6.75 oz)	25–30 min	$ .99	130	2	28	0
Barley Pilaf Mix*	6	1/2 c	177 g (6.25 oz)	35–40 min	$1.55	100	3	23	0

*Contains yeast extract or autolyzed yeast; see note regarding MSG in Chapter 2.

Product Notes:
Directions call for the addition of butter, but mixes can be made without it.

Comments:
The mixes are inexpensive and easy to use. All of them are improved by a sprinkling of grated cheese. Beware the MSG.

Nile Spice Foods, Inc.
119 West Denny Way #210
Seattle, WA 98119
(206) 281-7292

Nile Spice offers couscous mixes, rozdali (rice and lentil) mixes, soups, and seasonings. The company's Pack It Meals are designed for trail use.

Product	Serv per pkg	Serv size	Weight	Cooking time	Price	Cal	Pro Gm	Car Gm	Fat Gm
Lentil & Onion Couscous Pilaf	4	1/2 c	142 g (5 oz)	5 min	$1.50	153	4	25	4
Lemon Thyme Couscous Salad Mix	6	1/2 c	142 g (5 oz)	No cooking	$1.50	103	2	13	5
Vegetable Curry Rozdali	4	1/2 c	142 g (5 oz)	25 min	$1.50	154	6	25	4
Spicy Currant Rozdali	4	1/2 c	152 g (5.4 oz)	25 min	$1.50	161	5	27	4
Meals in a Cup									
Spicy Chili 'n Beans	1	7 fl oz	42 g (1.5 oz)	Add b. water	$1.30	160	10	30	1
Mild Chili 'n Beans	1	7 fl oz	42 g (1.5 oz)	Add b. water	$1.30	160	10	30	1
Primavera Pasta 'n Sauce	1	7 fl oz	53 g (1.9 oz)	Add b. water	$1.30	210	9	36	3
Mediterranean Pasta 'n Sauce	1	7 fl oz	53 g (1.9 oz)	Add b. water	$1.30	210	8	37	4
Parmesan Pasta 'n Sauce	1	7 fl oz	53 g (1.9 oz)	Add b. water	$1.30	210	9	36	4
Soups									
Tomato Minestrone Soup	1	10 fl oz	58 g (2 oz)	Add b. water	$1.30	200	9	41	0
Vegetable Parmesan Soup	1	10 fl oz	57 g (2 oz)	Add b. water	$1.30	200	9	35	3
Vegetable Chicken Soup	1	10 fl oz	57 g (2 oz)	Add b. water	$1.30	220	8	34	5
Lentil Curry Soup	1	10 fl oz	62 g (2.2 oz)	Add b. water	$1.30	220	10	44	Tr
Potato Romano Soup	1	10 fl oz	38 g (1.3 oz)	Add b. water	$1.30	150	5	24	5
Potato Leek Soup	1	10 fl oz	40 g (1.4 oz)	Add b. water	$1.30	160	4	25	5
Italian Tomato Soup	1	10 fl oz	40 g (1.4 oz)	Add b. water	$1.30	150	4	27	4
Pack It Meals	1	20 fl oz		Add b. water	$1.80	See Product Notes			

    Vegetable Chicken Soup
    Tomato Minestrone Soup
    Lentil Curry Soup
    Pasta Parmesan
    Original Chili
    Lentil Curry Soup

Product Notes:

Pack It Meals contain double portions of a soup or a Meal in a Cup, packaged in a paper envelope. Pack It Meals are available only through mail-order; contact the company for an order form. You can choose any assortment of Pack It Meals but must order in units of six. Prices are: 6–99 meals, $1.80 each; 100–199 meals, $1.20 each; 1000 + meals, $.90 each. Shipping is extra.

The two rozdali products and Lentil & Onion Couscous Pilaf require the addition of vegetable oil; Lemon Thyme Couscous Salad Mix requires olive oil, lemon juice, and tomato.

Nile Spice Foods sells six different seasoning products: Ginger Curry, Desert Spice, Nile Spice, Cleopatra's Secret, Seasoning of Garlic, and Lemon Pepper.

Comments:

The mixes are quite tasty. Couscous Pilaf is spicy without being overwhelming. Lemon Thyme Couscous Salad can be made with dehydrated tomatoes and lemon flavoring.

I found that the soups have more flavor than do the meals in a cup. Italian Tomato Soup and Lentil Curry Soup are especially good; the tomato soup is good by itself and would be good over rice or spaghetti. Chili 'n Beans— even the spicy version—is unexciting.

These products do not contain hydrolyzed vegetable protein, autolyzed yeast, or yeast extract, all of which contain MSG and "enhance" flavor. The trade-off when eating food without MSG may simply be that the food will not be quite as exciting.

At home, I use Nile Spice when I need to pep up a recipe; it is equally effective on trail. Lemon Pepper is nice on rehydrated vegetables, especially on a "salad" of tomatoes, cucumbers, green peppers, and onions.

Saco Foods Inc.
Madison, WI 53705

Saco Foods sells Cultured Buttermilk Blend, which is powdered buttermilk. Each can contains twenty-four servings (one serving is 3–4 tablespoons powder, which makes 1 cup buttermilk). The product is available in supermarkets and health-food stores. Buttermilk powder can be used to make buttermilk biscuits, buttermilk pancakes, and buttermilk chocolate cake. The price is $3.69 per can. Despite the name, the product is low in fat (3–4 tablespoons have 79 calories, 8 grams protein, 11 grams carbohydrate, and 1 gram fat).

The Spicery Shoppe
Flavorchem
1525 Brook Drive
Downers Grove, IL 60515
(708) 932-8100

The Spicery Shoppe offers a variety of all-natural, non-alcoholic flavors that are used in place of (alcohol) extracts. Flavors include: almond, anise, banana, black walnut, butter, cherry, cinnamon, coffee, lemon, maple, orange, peppermint, pineapple, strawberry, vanilla, and wintergreen. Each bottle contains 2 fluid ounces. Bottles need to be refrigerated after they are opened.

Comments:
I wanted to make Orange-Poppyseed Pancakes on trail but did not want to carry an orange and grater. I tried dehydrating orange rind, but it turned to cement and lost most of its flavor. I looked in vain for orange extract (as opposed to imitation orange extract) in my local supermarkets. Spicery Shoppe flavors, which are sold in health-food stores, fill the bill. The wide range of flavors covers almost every contingency. Instead of taking the whole bottle on trail, I put the desired amount in a film canister and seal it shut. These flavors are a wonderful way to add variety to trail recipes. Take some time to experiment with them and you will be rewarded.

Vogue Cuisine, Inc.
437 Golden Isles Drive
Hallandale, FL 33009
(305) 458-2915

Vogue Cuisine makes four soup bases: Instant Onion Base, Vege Base, Chicken Flavored Base, and Beef Flavored Base. Vege Base is vegetarian and salt-free; the other bases contain either chicken or beef products and are low-salt. The bases contain no artificial coloring, flavoring, or preservatives. All four soups, however, contain hydrolyzed vegetable protein; see note regarding MSG in Chapter 2. A 4-ounce jar contains 368 servings of 11 calories per serving. Suggested retail for a 4-ounce jar is $2.50. Vogue Cuisine products are available at health-food stores.

Comments:
Vege Base is bland because it's salt-free. The beef and chicken bases are flavorful, which is not surprising, because hydrolyzed vegetable protein is the first ingredient in each list.

Walnut Acres
Penns Creek, PA 17862
(717) 837-0603

Many Walnut Acres products are organic, and all are made without the use of chemical preservatives, additives, or flavorings. The company carries a huge line of products, including nut and fruit spreads, hot and cold cereals, sweeteners, whole grain mixes, dried fruits, nuts, snacks, grains, beans, seeds, flours, dried soup mixes, milk powder, soy beverage powder, and buttermilk powder. Walnut Acres products are available through natural-foods stores and mail-order. Contact the company for a catalog.

Product	Serv per pkg	Serv size	Weight	Cooking time	Price	Cal	Pro Gm	Car Gm	Fat Gm
12-Grain Cereal (about 4 c)	—	—	454 g (16 oz)	5–8 min	$2.45	Not available			
Raspberry Crunch Granola (about 4-1/2 c)	—	—	454 g (16 oz)	—	$3.99	Not available			
Tropical Trail Mix (about 3-1/2 c)	—	—	454 g (16 oz)	—	$6.99	Not available			
Sunshine Blend (about 8 c)	—	—	454 g (16 oz)	—	$7.15	Not available			
Peanut Butter	—	—	454 g (16 oz)	—	$3.99	Not available			
Cajun Rice (about 3-1/4 c dry)	—	—	454 g (16 oz)	40–50 min	$3.49	Not available			
Split Pea & Barley Soup (about 2-3/4 c dry)	—	—	454 g (16 oz)	40–50 min	$3.89	Not available			
Fruitcake	—	—	907 g (32 oz)	—	$14.59	Not available			

Comments:
These products are terrific. The Cajun Rice was worth the forty-minute wait. The trail mixes are a nice change from gorp. The Raspberry Granola tasted like it contained real raspberries rather than imitations. The fruitcake is marvelous.

Williams Foods, Inc.
13301 West 99th Street
Lenexa, KS 66215
(913) 888-4343

Williams Foods offers several seasoning mixes (Chili, Turkey Chili, Sloppy Joe, and Taco) that can be used as directed (with meat) or with dehydrated or freeze-dried beans. Packets cost sixty-seven to ninety-five cents each for 28 to 39 grams of seasoning. These seasonings are available in supermarkets. Taco Seasoning contains hydrolyzed vegetable protein; see note regarding MSG in Chapter 2.

10
Complementary Proteins

Protein is made up of twenty-two amino acids, eight of which are considered essential because they cannot be manufactured in the body and must be obtained from food. The human body needs these building blocks in certain proportions: One unit of tryptophan must be present with 3.2 units of lysine and 4.3 units of leucine, and so on. The body also needs these essential amino acids at the same time, so foods providing these building blocks must be eaten at the same meal or no more than a few hours apart.

If food has only one-half unit of tryptophan, then the body can use only one and a half units of isoleucine and two units of leucine, regardless of how much isoleucine or leucine is present. The extra amino acids cannot be stored for future tissue-building, so they are burned for energy.

The amino acid pattern in chicken eggs most closely duplicates the amino acid pattern needed by humans. Over 94 percent of the protein in chicken eggs is "usable"; the remaining 6 percent is burned or stored as fat. Over 80 percent of the protein in milk, 80 percent of the protein in fish, 70 to 75 percent of the protein in cheese, and

65 to 70 percent of the protein in meat and poultry is usable by humans.

Grains, legumes, nuts, and seeds also contain protein, though they are each deficient in one or more of the essential amino acids. For example, only 42 percent of the protein in peanut butter and 30 percent of the protein in lentils is usable.

If you drink a glass of milk when you eat half a cup of rice, the milk will supply the missing isoleucine and lysine in the rice and increase its usable protein by almost a third. This principle holds true for other foods as well. By matching the amino acid strengths and weaknesses of various foods, you can use complementary relationships to increase the amount of usable protein in grains, legumes, and nuts. In general, the following combinations have strong complementary relationships: milk products and grains, legumes and grains, and legumes and seeds.

Quick Complements and the Protein They Add

If you do not want to spend a lot of time carefully calculating complementarity but you would like the extra protein that comes from combining amino acids, use the following chart to plan complements at each meal. Many complements—such as cereal and milk, pasta and cheese, and beans and cheese—are already a part of our diet. My source of information for the following charts is Frances Moore Lappé's *Diet for a Small Planet,* 20th Anniversary Edition.

Quick Complements

Food	Portion	Grams protein gained	Quick complement
Grains			
Barley	1/2 c dry	2	1 T soy grits or scant
Bulgur	1/2 c dry	1.5	3 T instant powdered
Millet	1/2 c dry	1.1	milk or 3 T grated cheese

Quick Complements *(continued)*

Food	Portion	Grams protein gained	Quick complement
Grains (continued)			
Oatmeal	1/2 c dry	1.9	1 T soy grits or scant 3 T instant powdered milk or 3 T grated cheese
Rice, brown	1/2 c dry	2	,,
Rice, white	1/2 c dry	1.9	,,
Rye, grain	1/2 c dry	1.9	,,
Wheat, flour	1 c	2	,,
Wheat, grain	1/2 c dry	1.9	,,
Wheat, cracked	1/2 c dry	2	,,
Wheat, cream of	3/4 c cooked	1.3	,,
Wheat, macaroni	1/2 c dry	0.7	,,
Wheat, spaghetti	1/2 c dry	1	,,
Beans, Peas, Peanuts			
Beans (navy, black, kidney, lima)	1/2 c dry	4.2	1/4 c egg powder or 6 T grated cheese or 1/3 c instant powdered milk or 3/4 c sunflower or sesame seeds
Lentils	1/2 c dry	4.2	,,
Peas (dry split, chick)	1/2 c dry	4.2	,,
Soybeans or grits	1/2 c dry	3.9	,,
Soy flour	1 c	5	,,
Peanuts	1/4 c nuts or 1/8 c butter	1.1	1 T instant powdered milk

Nondairy Complements

If you do not eat dairy products, use the following chart to assemble complementary portions. Beans, rice, soy grits, and bulgur are given as cooked portions.

1/2 c rice : 3 T beans[1]
1/2 c rice : 1 T soy grits
1/2 c rice : 3/8 c bulgur : 1/3 c soy grits
1/2 c rice : 1-1/2 T sesame butter[2]
1/2 c bulgur : 2 scant T beans
1/2 c bulgur : 2 T soy grits

1/2 c bulgur : 1 T soy grits : 2 T sesame seeds
1/2 c flour : 1 T soy grits
1-1/2 c peanuts : 2/3 c soybeans : 1-3/4 c sesame seeds
3/4 c peanuts : 1 c sesame or sunflower seeds
1 c cornmeal : 1/4 c beans
1/2 c beans : 1/2 c sesame seeds

[1]Split peas and lentils have roughly the same amino acid pattern as beans and can be substituted for them.
[2]Sunflower seeds have roughly the same amino acid pattern as sesame seeds and can be substituted for them.

Equivalent Quantities

Use these equivalent quantities if you are substituting one form of a food for another.

1/2 c soybeans	= 1/2 c soy grits
	1 scant c soy flour
	17 oz tofu
1/3 c instant nonfat dry milk	= 1 c liquid milk
	1/4 c noninstant nonfat dry milk
	1/3 c grated cheese (packed)
	1 oz cheese
1/8 c peanut butter	= 1/4 c peanuts
1 c whole wheat flour	= 3/4 c bulgur
	1/2 c wheat berries
	1 c rolled grain
	5 slices commercial bread
	1 c pasta (dry)
1/2 c sesame seeds	= 1/4 c sesame butter
1 c cornmeal	= 6–7 cornmeal tortillas

11
Expedition
Food Lists

On July 1, 1975, five friends and I flew to Ivanhoe Lake near the headwaters of the Dubawnt River in the Northwest Territories of Canada. In the seven weeks that followed, we traveled almost 800 miles by canoe through northern boreal forest and tundra. The trip thoroughly tested the tenets of what came to be *The Healthy Trail Food Book,* my original cookbook. Except for fish and berries, we carried all of our food with us and depended on it for health and sustenance.

The menu was simple. There were four different breakfasts coupled with four dinners; lunch was the same every day. We carried enough staples to improvise quite a bit, but the meals themselves were easy to prepare after a hard day. Rice for dinner every fourth day may sound tiresome, but trail life is uncomplicated and so were our tastes.

We carried approximately 2 pounds of food per person per day, totaling almost 600 pounds. The only perishables were cheese, margarine, and onions. Though I had packed Parmesan cheese for the last two weeks and had allotted no margarine for that time, we had extra Cheddar and margarine through the end of the trip and both lasted well.

Because we were concerned about the lack of firewood on the tundra, I milled one-fourth of the dinner meals to reduce cooking time and we often made muesli from oatmeal breakfasts to save wood and gas.

The only items we obtained through trail-food suppliers were tomato crystals, sour cream powder, powdered eggs, dehydrated onions, and dehydrated peppers. We purchased all other food from co-ops, wholesalers, and supermarkets.

The following list details the food we packed. I have made a few changes in amounts, decreasing sugar and powdered milk (of which we had too much) and increasing tomato crystals (of which we had not enough). I planned 2/3 cup dry grain per person for breakfast and only 1/3 cup dry grain per person for dinner. This strategy gave us more food when we needed it—at the beginning of the day. However, we often saved some Biscuit Mix to supplement dinner and I now normally plan larger portions for dinner.

We averaged 3,735 calories (with 36 percent of those calories from fats) and 74.7 grams of usable complemented protein per person per day. Though we could have made some small changes, the six of us were satisfied with the quantity and quality of the food.

For the seven-week trip, we packed: forty-nine cloth bags of food, each containing food for one day; a spice bag; a pantry bag that contained tomato crystals, coffee, and so on; and bulk-packed items such as margarine, peanut butter, shortening, and honey.

Dubawnt River Trip

Food for one day (dry portion)	Per person per day (as prepared)	Total quantity for trip
General		
18 envelopes cocoa	3 c cocoa	882 envelopes
6 teabags		392 teabags
1 lb Biscuit Mix		49 lbs
1-1/2 c brown sugar	2 T	74 cups (37 lbs)
2 c powdered milk		98 cups (20 lbs)

(Continued on next page)

Dubawnt River Trip *(continued)*

Food for one day (dry portion)	Per person per day (as prepared)	Total quantity for trip
Breakfast		
#1: 4 c bulgur	2/3 c	52 c (26 lbs)
#2: 4 c rolled oats and wheat	2/3 c	48 c (10 lbs)
#3: 4 c rolled rye and sunflower seeds	2/3 c	48 c (10 lbs)
#4: 6 c granola	1 c	72 c (about 20 lbs)
Lunch		
1 lb cheese	2-2/3 oz	49 lbs
1 lb nuts	2-2/3 oz	49 lbs
1 lb raisins	2-2/3 oz	49 lbs
1 lb dried fruit	2-2/3 oz	49 lbs
6 oz chocolate bits	1 oz	about 7 lbs
6 oz lemonade mix	1-1/2 c	about 7 lbs
Dinner		
#1: 2 c lentils or millet	1/3 c	24 c (12 lbs)
#2: 2 c grain mix or chili	1/3 c	24 c (12 lbs)
#3: 3 c split peas	1/2 c	36 c (18 lbs)
#4: 2 c rice	1/3 c	24 c (12 lbs)

Additional food
Bulk-packed food

Margarine, 1 c per day except last 2 weeks	33 c (16 lbs)
Shortening, 1 c per day	49 c (25 lbs)
Peanut butter, 1/2 c per day	25 c (12-1/2 lbs)
Honey	1 gallon
17 desserts (one every three days	
8" layer cake mix	3 mixes
egg custard (1-1/2 qt)	7 bags
pudding (1 qt)	7 bags

Pantry items

Sour cream powder	#10 can
Tomato crystals	#10 can
Dehydrated onions	4 c
Dehydrated peppers	3 c
Powdered eggs	#10 can

(Continued on next page)

Dubawnt River Trip *(continued)*

Food for one day *(dry portion)*	*Per person per day* *(as prepared)*	*Total quantity for trip*
Pantry items (Continued)		
Extra Biscuit Mix		5 lbs
Cornmeal		4 lbs
Yeast		10 packets
Coffee		2 large jars instant
		3 lbs ground
Lemon juice		3 plastic lemons
Onions		10 lbs
Soup		25 envelopes (1-1/2 c per envelope)
		1/2 c soup base
Bouillon: beef, chicken, and onion		1 jar each
Fig bars		2 packages
Spices		
Salt		2 lbs
Pepper		2 c
Garlic powder		1 large jar
Onion powder		1 small jar
Curry		1/2 c
Chili powder		1/3 c
Chili peppers		1 small jar
Tomato sauce spices		3 c
Parsley		2 c
Cayenne		1 small can
Cinnamon		2 large jars
Indian seasonings (premeasured for lemon rice)		3 meals' worth
Nutmeg		1 small jar

The Moisie River Trip

Four years later, in July 1979, three friends and I left for a sixteen-day canoe trip on the Moisie River in Quebec. Lunch consisted of bannock, nuts, fruit, peanut butter, honey, and cheese. Having had my fill of split pea soup, and lentil stew on the Dubawnt, I tried some new dinners and desserts. We used a pressure cooker for beans and grains and a frying pan with a lid for baking.

Quiche and trail enchiladas were wonderful but required lots of time and infinite patience, so they did not make it into the revised edition of the cookbook. One of our group was from New Mexico and brought a dozen cans of green chilies. We had green chilies and cheese, green chilies and bread, green chilies and enchiladas, and green chilies and chili. It was the Mexican Moisie trip.

Moisie River Trip

	Breakfast	Lunch	Dinner
Day 1	Granola	See text	Carrow-Cashew Soup, crackers
Day 2	Bulgur	Same	Spaghetti, Date-nut Bars
Day 3	Spiced Fruit Rice Pudding	Same	Cheddar Cheese Chowder
Day 4	Granola	Same	Cheddar Cheese Chowder, tapioca pudding
Day 5	Bulgur	Same	Lentils with green chilies, tortillas
Day 6	Oatmeal	Same	Baked beans, tortillas
Day 7	Granola	Same	Quiche, trout
Day 8	Bulgur	Same	Mexican Oatmeal Soup, trail enchiladas
Day 9	Oatmeal	Same	Split Pea Soup, brownies
Day 10	Granola	Same	Curried Rice
Day 11	Bulgur	Same	Alpine Rice
Day 12	Spiced Fruit Rice Pudding	Same	Macaroni and Cheese, Date Pudding
Day 13	Granola	Same	Chili, gingerbread
Day 14	Bulgur	Same	Mexican Oatmeal Soup, Parsley Rice
Day 15	Oatmeal	Same	Risi e Bisi
Day 16	Bulgur	Same	Fresh food!

The Harricanaw River Trip

When I began working on this book, I scheduled several trips to review food and test new recipes. One trip turned into a mini-expedition as three friends and I headed north for ten days on the Harricanaw River, which runs into James Bay. On the Harricanaw we discovered huge falls, challenging rapids, low water levels, and few good campsites. We got up early and often paddled until 8:00 P.M.; we gained an appreciation for tasty, quick-cooking, easy-to-prepare food. At the end of the trip we had extra dried fruit, nuts, and other lunch items; I had packed enough for four hungry men instead of four hungry women.

Harricanaw River Trip

	Breakfast	Lunch	Dinner
Day 1	—	(Below)	Shrimp Cantonese, Oriental Sweet and Sour, fig bars
Day 2	12-grain Cereal with dried fruit and milk	Same	Spaghetti with tomato sauce and Parmesan cheese, fig bars
Day 3	Bear Mush with dried fruit and milk	Same	Summer Chicken, Santa Fe Chicken, Fruitcake
Day 4	7-Grain Cereal with dried fruit and milk	Same	Cajun Rice, Carrot Cake
Day 5	Scrambled eggs, Mexican Omelette, Blueberry Muffins	Same	Santa Fe Black Beans and Rice, Big Bill's Beans and Rice, fig bars and fruitcake
Day 6	Raspberry Crunch Granola with milk	Same	Mediterranean Pasta, Zucchini Lasagna
Day 7	Honey Almond Granola with milk	Same	Wild Rice with Vegetables, Rice Pilaf
Day 8	Almond-Date Rice Cereal with milk	Same	Couscous Almondine, Curried Vegetables with Couscous
Day 9	Homebody Posole Chili	Same	Buckwheat pancakes and maple syrup
Day 10	Fried bulgur	Same	Green Pea and Barley Soup, Cornbread

(Continued on next page)

Harricanaw River Trip *(continued)*

Lunch:

For trip:
2 loaves of bread
3 Biscuit Mixes
Carrots
1 jar of homemade blackberry jam
1 jar of peanut butter
For each day:
2-1/2 c mixed nuts
1-1/2 c mixed dried fruit
1/2 lb cheese
1-1/2 c raisins
5 four-inch strips beef jerky
4 snack bars
1/2 large chocolate bar
Lemonade

Pantry:
10 oz cooking oil
10 oz honey
1 lb flour
Bouillon, 6 pkg instant soup
1 c margarine
1 c sour cream powder
1-1/2 c Parmesan cheese
1 c homemade maple syrup
1 lb brown sugar
3 c powdered milk
Salt, cinnamon, garlic powder
Extra dehydrated vegetables
Hot chocolate, coffee
Bengal Spice, Earl Grey teas
Emergency food

Resources

Books

Alternative Pioneering. *Harvest Maid: The Complete Guide to Food Dehydrating.* Chaska, Minn.: Alternative Pioneering, n.d.

Brody, Jane. *Jane Brody's Good Food Book.* New York: Bantam Books, 1985.

———. *Jane Brody's Nutrition Book.* New York: W. W. Norton & Company, 1981.

Corbin, Charles B., and Ruth Lindsey. *Fitness for Life.* 2d ed. Glenview, Ill.: Scott, Foresman & Co., 1985.

Ewald, Ellen Buchman. *Recipes for a Small Planet.* New York: Ballantine Books, 1973.

Ferber, Peggy. *Mountaineering: The Freedom of the Hills.* Seattle: The Mountaineers, 1974.

Gunn, Carolyn. *The Expedition Cookbook.* Denver, Colo.: Chockstone Press, Inc., 1988.

Jacobson, Michael F. *The Complete Eater's Digest and Nutrition Scoreboard.* New York: Anchor Press/Doubleday, 1985.

Lappé, Frances Moore. *Diet for a Small Planet.* 20th ann. ed. New York: Ballantine Books, 1991.

Latimer, Carole. *Wilderness Cuisine: How to Prepare and Enjoy Fine Food on the Trail and in Camp.* Berkeley, Calif.: Wilderness Press, 1991.

Pennington, Jean A. T. *Food Values of Portions Commonly Used.* New York: HarperCollins Publishers, 1989.

Spangenberg, Jean. *BakePacker Companion.* Whittier, N.C.: Adventure Foods, 1992. (BakePacker cookbook)

Sukey, Richard, Donna Orr, and Claudia Lindholm. *NOLS Cookery.* Harrisburg, Pa.: Stackpole Books and National Outdoor Leadership School, 1988.

U.S. Department of Agriculture. *Nutritive Value of American Foods in Common Units.* Agriculture Handbook no. 456. Washington, D.C.: GPO, 1988.

——. *Nutritive Value of Foods.* Home and Garden Bulletin no. 72. Washington, D.C.: GPO, 1971.

Organizations

Center for Science in the Public Interest (CSPI). A nonprofit public-interest membership organization that advocates improved health and nutrition practices. Publishes "Nutrition Action Health Letter," wall charts, a pocket-sized list of additives to avoid, and other consumer publications. 1875 Connecticut Avenue N.W., Suite 300, Washington, D.C. 20009-5728; (202) 332-9110.

National Organization Mobilized to Stop Glutamate (NO MSG). A nonprofit membership organization concerned with the use of MSG in foods. Works to change labeling laws and publishes a quarterly newsletter. P.O. Box 367, Santa Fe, New Mexico 87504; 1 (800) 288-0718.

Products

BakePacker. Strike 2 Industries, Inc., E. 508 Augusta Avenue, Spokane, Washington 99207; (509) 484-3701. Available in outdoor stores across the country.

Harvest Maid Food Dehydrator. Alternative Pioneering Systems, Inc., P.O. Box 159, Chaska, Minnesota 55318; (612) 448-4400. Contact for information about local retailers.

Outback Oven and accessories. Traveling Light, Inc., 1563 Solano Avenue, Suite 284, Berkeley, California 94707; (510) 526-8401. Available in outdoor stores across the country; call or write for product brochure.

Wood-burning stoves. Z.Z. Corp, 10806 Kaylor Street, Los Alamitos, California 90720; (310) 598-3220. Also carries pot sets and other accessories. Available in outdoor stores across the country; call or write for a product brochure.

Index